OUR LADY IN THE LITURGY

OUR LADY
in the
LITURGY

by

Dom E. Flicoteaux, o.s.b.

Translated by Dom Aldhelm Dean, o.s.b.

1959
HELICON PRESS
BALTIMORE   MARYLAND

Originally published in French under the title
Mystères et Fêtes de la Vierge Marie
by Les Editions du Cerf

Imprimi potest: ✠ fr. M. Gabriel Tissot
Abbot of Quarr
15 Novembris, 1958

Nihil obstat: Dermitius Fogarty, D.D.
Censor deputatus

Imprimatur: ✠ Cyrillus
Episcopus Southwarcensis

Library of Congress Catalog Card No. 59-13369

PRINTED IN GREAT BRITAIN
FOR HELICON PRESS, INC.
5305 EAST DRIVE, BALTIMORE, 27, MD.

CONTENTS

PART TWO

FEASTS INSTITUTED IN HONOUR OF THE BLESSED VIRGIN

Many footnotes in the original of this work, *Mystères et Fêtes de la Vierge Marie*, have been included in the text in this translation wherever possible. A few, of minor importance, that had exclusive bearing on conditions in France, have been omitted. We wish to thank Messrs Burns Oates & Washbourne for permission to use a few quotations from their *Roman Missal*.

FOREWORD

THE essential purpose of the liturgical cycle, as constituted by the Church, is to make us live over again, year by year, the work of our redemption in the successive phases of its development, from the coming of the Word into the world until the outpouring of the Holy Spirit on the day of Pentecost, and so to bring us on our way to the coming of Christ in glory, the supreme object of our sojourn here below. It is true that, in the course of the liturgical year, the Church celebrates not only the mysteries of our Saviour's life for us, but also the feast-days of the saints now reigning with him in heaven. Nevertheless we must make no mistake; in celebrating the saints, it is Christ himself in them that the Church celebrates, Christ the author and the model of all holiness. The liturgy of All Saints is especially significant in this connection. Is it not presented to us with the 'Lamb as it were slain' as the centre of all? The Lamb that has conquered by his blood and is now enthroned in the heights of heaven, surrounded by the multitude of saints that owe their sharing in his glory to him alone. Furthermore, we honour the saints not only because the virtue of Christ shines in them according to the degree of their fidelity to his example, but also because they all had a share, each following his personal vocation, in the work of our redemption. If a few of them, like John the Baptist and the Apostles, were privileged to co-operate directly with Jesus himself during his earthly mission, all the others have done no more, in the course of the centuries, than carry on the work started by Christ, devoting themselves to the building up of the Church and preparing the final coming of his kingdom.

Now if the cultus given to the saints is exalted in proportion to the depth and intimacy of their co-operation with the work of our Saviour, both on earth and in heaven, it is easy to understand the exceptional place given, in the liturgical year, to the Mother of the Redeemer, the Blessed Virgin Mary. Pius XII has declared, 'Among all the saints in heaven, the Blessed Virgin Mary, Mother of God, is the object of our deepest veneration. For indeed, because of her God-given mission, her life is closely bound up with the mysteries of Christ, and certainly nobody ever followed in the footsteps of the Incarnate Word more faithfully or effectively; nobody enjoys greater favour or greater power than she with the most sacred Heart of the Son of God and, through him, with the Heavenly Father.'[1]

Since the cultus of the Virgin Mother is set before us as, so to speak, the indispensable complement of the cultus rendered to her Son, it is not surprising that, during the first Christian centuries, the Roman Church felt no need to celebrate the Blessed Virgin otherwise than through her participation in the mysteries of Christ. As Neubert, in his *Marie dans l'Eglise anténicéene* (1908), so justly says, 'The image of Mary was not set before the gaze of the faithful of those days in the same way as were those of other saints. For them, the culminating point of their life, the very thing which stirred up the pious veneration of the faithful, their martyrdom, attracted attention prior to their union with Christ. Each saint was a separate individual, bearing witness indeed for Christ, but evoking the thought of Christ only in a secondary manner. It was perfectly natural then to pay them special honour. Mary, on the hand, has no meaning apart from Jesus. In her conception of the Divine Word, in visiting Elizabeth, in giving birth to her son, in treating with the shepherds and the Wise Men, with Simeon in the temple, at Nazareth, at Cana, at the foot of the Cross, everywhere throughout the Gospel she is inseparably united to Jesus . . . her mysteries are the mysteries of Jesus, her glory is the reflection of his glory. Whenever the Son is honoured, the Mother is honoured too.'

There is little ground, therefore, for the reproach sometimes levelled at the Roman Church, that she waited until the sixth

1 Encyclical Mediator Dei.

or seventh century before celebrating the Virgin Mother in her liturgy, thus letting herself be forestalled by the Eastern Churches, from whom she received her earliest feasts of our Lady. In actual fact, the Roman Church has never been in need of encouragement or foreign influence in the matter of her cultus offered to the Mother of God. From her very earliest days, she has always shown forth a most delicate and virile devotion towards the Mother of Christ, but with that sobriety and discretion so characteristic of the early Roman liturgy,[2] and with theological import peculiarly her own.

This little work which we now offer to the ever growing liturgical library consists of two parts. In the first part (the more important, in our opinion), we shall stress the celebration of the Mother of Christ as one who shares directly in the mysteries of our salvation. This first part deserves the more to hold our attention since one cannot fail to notice in certain modern authors a regrettable tendency to 'separate the Blessed Virgin Mary from those theological realities in the midst of which she stands' (Laurentin, *Maria*, t. III, p. 735). In the second part of this work, we shall consider our Lady as presented in those feasts that the Church has instituted more especially in her honour, but always bearing in mind the privileged part she plays in the work of our redemption.

Abbaye Sainte-Marie des Deux-Montagnes, Canada.
Low Sunday, 17th April, 1955.

2 cf. Ed. Bishop, *Liturgica Historica.*

PART ONE
MARY IN THE MYSTERIES OF OUR SALVATION

CHAPTER I

CHRISTMAS, THE PERFECT FEAST OF THE VIRGIN MOTHER

THE BLESSED VIRGIN, MOTHER OF GOD'S SON

EACH of the many feasts of our Lady that succeed one another in the course of the liturgical year brings us some special light, some special joy. Nevertheless, is it not true to say that among these feasts, the most fruitful, the ones that make the greatest appeal to our filial piety, are those in which the Virgin Mother and her divine Son are set before us as inseparably united in the realization of some mystery in which they both share, and for which the Church embraces them both in one act of praise? Granted so much, the feast celebrated on December 25th has exceptional interest for us, for nowhere is the Mother of God found more closely united to her Son in the work of our salvation than on that 'most blessed day', on which, according to one of those admirable formulas of which the Church has the secret and which go back to her earliest days, the Christian world emphatically declares that it is celebrating the inviolable virginity of Blessed Mary as she gives birth to the Saviour of the world: *Diem sacratissimum celebrantes quo beatae Mariae virginitas huic mundo edidit Salvatorem* (*Communicantes* of the Canon of the Mass).

Christmas is not only the oldest festival in which the Roman Church honours the Blessed Virgin Mary as Mother of God, the Θεοτόκος, but still remains today the most perfect feast of the divine maternity. Other feasts of our Lady, the Purification, the Annunciation, the Assumption and the Nativity, were unknown in Rome before the end of the seventh century. Bossuet does not hesitate to say that in giving birth to the Son of God according to the flesh, the Blessed

Virgin became in a certain manner, by the power of God himself, 'associated with his eternal generation'. Discerning in the virginal birth of our Saviour a certain reflection of his divine generation, the Bishop of Meaux goes so far as to say that 'God sent forth into the Virgin's womb something of that love that he has for his Son'. Indeed, we willingly apply to the bodily birth of Mary's Son certain texts of the Christmas liturgy which envisage more directly the eternal birth of the Son of God *in sinu Patris*.

Of course it is only natural that the Christmas liturgy should concentrate our attention on the person of Christ, whose birth the Church is celebrating, but not without a shining ray of divine light falling upon the Virgin who brought him into the world. Moreover, in this office of the Nativity, the union between Christ and his Mother is so close that our praises cannot reach the new-born Son of God without at the same time embracing that Blessed Maid whose name springs so readily to our lips, each time we give glory to the three divine Persons:

> *Gloria tibi Domine*
> *Qui natus es de Virgine*
> *Cum Patre et Sancto Spiritu*
> *In sempiterna saecula.*
> Eternal glory ever be
> O Lord, the Virgin-born, to thee
> Whom with the Father we adore
> And Holy Spirit evermore.

This doxology which ends the hymns on all feasts of our Lady is surely pre-eminently suitable for the Christmas season.

The place chosen for the solemn celebration of our Lord's birth is the most splendid sanctuary raised in honour of the Mother of God by the city of Rome, St Mary Major's. This great basilica, founded by Pope Liberius and re-built by Sixtus III not long after the Council of Ephesus (431), was dedicated to Mary, Mother of God, and received the name of *Basilica Sanctae Mariae*. It is not the oldest, but certainly is the greatest and most sumptuous of the Roman churches dedi-

cated to the Virgin Mother. Since there was in this church an
oratory representing the place of our Saviour's birth, it
became known as *Sancta Maria ad praesepe*, St Mary of the
Crib, and became for the faithful of Rome a representation of
Bethlehem just as the church of the Holy Cross was a representation of Jerusalem. In former days, the Pope would
preside in person at the greater part of the office of Christmas
in St Mary Major's, and, as we may see in our missals, it is
still in this church that the two 'Station' Masses of Christmas
are celebrated, that of the night and that of the day. In
primitive times the Mass of the day was celebrated at St
Peter's, but in the twelfth century it was transferred to St
Mary Major's *'propter parvitatem dici et difficultatem viae'* (*Ordo
Romanus* XI, 17). In the first Mass of Christmas, the Gospel
tells of the birth of the Blessed Mother's *primogenitus*; in the
second, that of the dawn, we are invited to join the shepherds
of Bethlehem in adoring the Saviour. In each of these two
Masses, the Mother of Christ is found quite naturally in the
forefront of the mystery, sharing the homage that we offer to
her Son.

As for the Christmas night office (Matins and Lauds), whose
splendour there is no need to emphasize here, the Church is
not content simply to celebrate the glory of the Word made
flesh, but with lyrical delicacy she sings also the praises of the
divine maternity united to virginity. Of the eight responses
found in the Roman office, the Church consecrates no less
than four to the Virgin Mother. Impossible to gauge ade-
quately the Church's delight in showing forth the part
played by the Blessed Virgin in this mystery of Christmas. In
the fourth of these responses, *O magnum mysterium*, she boldly
proclaims 'the Virgin was indeed blessed, whose womb was
found worthy to bear the Lord Christ', *Beata Virgo, cujus
viscera meruerunt portare Dominum Christum*. Once she has
become Mother of God, the Virgin Mary appears so exalted
above all creatures of heaven and earth that the Church feels
herself incapable of proclaiming such glory:

Holy and immaculate virginity, I know not how to

praise thee worthily, for him whom neither heaven nor earth can contain, him thou didst bear in thy womb. Blessed art thou among women and blessed is the fruit of thy womb.

Sancta et immaculata virginitas, quibus te laudibus efferam nescio, quia quem coeli capere non poterant tuo gremio contulisti. V. Benedicta tu in mulieribus et benedictus fructus ventris tui.

This response is used for other feasts of our Lady also, but its proper place is as the sixth response of the Roman Christmas Matins. In the *Revue Grégorienne* (November-December 1948), Dom Gajard gives some excellent commentaries on the Christmas responses, both as regards their text and their melody. He considers the one quoted above as the masterpiece of the whole second nocturn of Christmas.

Another response, which no longer is to be found in the Roman office, but has been preciously preserved in Benedictine and Dominican liturgical books, sings of the mysterious marriage of the Divine Word with humanity in that nuptial chamber that was the Virgin's womb:

He came down from heaven, true God born of the Father; he entered into the Virgin's womb, so as to become visible to our eyes, by clothing himself in human flesh born of our first father; then he came forth through the closed door, God and man, light and life, the world's Creator.

Such is the text of the fourth response of Christmas Matins in the monastic office. In the monastic Processional an older version is to be found, containing interesting variations. No doubt it was the acrimonious criticism to which this earlier version was subjected by certain writers of the Middle Ages, notably Agobard, Archbishop of Lyons, in his *Liber de correctione antiphonarii* (P.L. 104, 332), which discredited the older version and caused it to be substituted by the later edition.

Writing of this response as now found in the monastic office, Dom Gajard says (*op. cit.*), 'Here all is clarity, shining light, freshness, virginal purity, serenity—in a word *beauty* in the fullest meaning of the word'. Indeed, it would be impossible to sing in more expressive phrases the great mystery of the divine maternity.

We must not fail to notice either, in this Christmas office, what care the Church takes to preserve youthful freshness and simplicity in her portrayal of our Lady. In this connection, nothing is more characteristic than the Lauds hymn, *A solis ortus cardine*, written by the poet Sedulius, whose first verses tell of the Virgin Mother:

> Afar from where the sun doth rise
> To lands beneath the western skies,
> Homage to Christ our King we pay,
> Born of a Virgin's womb this day.

> Blessed Creator, thou didst take
> A servant's likeness for our sake,
> And didst in flesh our flesh restore
> To bid thy creature live once more.

> Chaste was the womb where thou didst dwell
> Of heavenly grace the hidden cell;
> Nor might the blessed Maid proclaim
> Whence her dread Guest in secret came.

> Down from on high God came to rest
> His glory in a sinless breast;
> Obedience at his word believed,
> And virgin innocence conceived.

> Ere long, that holy Child she bore,
> By Gabriel's message named before,
> Whom, yet unborn, with eager pride,
> The swift forerunner prophesied.

(Trans. R. A. Knox, in *New Westminster Hymnal*. No. 8.)

In the original Latin, the last line of the third verse, *Secreta*, *quae non noverat*, has caused no small embarrassment to commentators and translators. Obviously, once she had conceived the Saviour, our Lady could not be ignorant of the mystery she bore in her womb. Had not the angel Gabriel revealed to her what was to be accomplished in her and the miraculous nature of her conceiving? The 'unknown mystery' must therefore refer to the special grace poured out upon our Lady to prepare her for her divine conception. Before conceiving the Saviour, the Blessed Virgin bore within her the mystery of which she was as yet ignorant. Such an interpretation seems reasonable enough when we remember that here the poet follows events in their chronological order. The fourth verse tells of the conception, the fifth of the birth, the sixth of what followed after the birth, etc.

The second antiphon at Lauds is also borrowed from this hymn of Sedulius, and the Gregorian melody composed for it brings out most strikingly its exquisite suavity:

> The Mother has given birth to the King, whose name is eternal; she has both a Mother's joy and a Virgin's privilege; not one has ever been, or shall ever be like her. Alleluia.

There is nothing formal or stiff in this Christmas office; all is living, alert and joyful. We are still far from those modern compositions whose heavy style and insipid sentimentality only too often produces nothing but boredom and uneasiness.

The Blessed Virgin, Mother of the Saviour

Christmas celebrates the Son of God being born into this world as our Saviour, the Saviour promised and expected for centuries past. The joyful news that the angels hasten to announce to the shepherds of Bethlehem is precisely this fact, that their Saviour has just been born: *Quia natus est vobis Salvator qui est Christus Dominus* (Luke 2, 11). Making use of the words of St Leo, the Church delights in celebrating Christmas Day as the day of our redemption: *Hodie illuxit nobis dies redemptionis novae, reparationis antiquae.* The Church never loses sight of the unity of the work of our redemption, and so, in more than one of her liturgical formulas, she speaks as though Christ had already saved the world by his birth alone (cf. Collect for Christmas Day). It is only natural, therefore, that the Christmas liturgy should emphasize the fact that the Blessed Virgin is Mother of our Saviour. In one of the responses of the night office, the Church proclaims with conviction:

> Blessed is Mary, Mother of God, whose womb remains inviolate; it is today that she brought forth the Saviour of the world (5th response).

In the seventh response, the Church reminds us, with consummate discretion, that the virginal birth itself is an integral part of the work of our redemption:

> Blessed is the womb of the Virgin Mary that bore the Son of the eternal Father, and blessed are the breasts that fed Christ the Lord, even he who, on this day, deigned to be born of the Virgin for the salvation of the world.

Artists of the Middle Ages gave their support to this idea, that on Christmas Day our Lady gave us the Victim of our salvation, the true Lamb of God, by representing the divine Infant lying, not in a crib, but on an altar, while the Blessed Virgin his mother lies down near him (cf. Emile Male. *L'Art religieux du XIIIe siècle en France*, p. 221).

Let us add that, not content with honouring the Blessed Virgin as Mother of God and Mother of the Saviour on Christmas Day, the Church invites us to recognize her and love her already as one who will become our own Mother. For the Child to whom Mary gives birth and whom she wraps so tenderly in swaddling clothes, is, as the Gospel tells us (Luke 2, 7; Rom. 8, 29), the first-born of her sons: *Et peperit Filium suum primogenitum*. This text, without in any way giving countenance to heretical ideas which would have it that our Lady gave birth to other children after Jesus, does forcibly suggest nevertheless that the Blessed Virgin was to become, in future generations, the mother of an ample spiritual posterity of which Christ was the first-born. So when the Blessed Mother contemplated her only Son, the object of all her love, lying in the manger, she surely must have realized that in giving birth to him, she had brought forth the head of that great family which, through all future generations, would proclaim her blessed.

Consequently, if we really wish to live over again the mystery of Christmas as we should, and profit by the special grace it brings us year by year, let us not fail to place ourselves under the protection of the Blessed Virgin as our own Mother. She knows how to awake in us those same dispositions of tenderness and filial openness as were those of Christ Jesus, when, like a fruit fully ripe, he came forth from her virginal womb.

CHAPTER II

THE OCTAVE DAY OF CHRISTMAS

THE OFFICE AND MASS FOR JANUARY 1ST

FEELING, no doubt, that she has not yet paid our Lady, on Christmas Day itself, such special honours as are due to her virginal maternity, the Roman Church lost no time in instituting a feast more especially reserved to the Mother of God. Officially, it is true, the Church celebrates the Circumcision of our Lord eight days after Christmas. However, neither the office nor the Mass for January 1st has much to say about this mystery. In the Mass, only the very short Gospel alludes to it at all. In the office, only the lessons of the first nocturn and the homily of St Ambrose on the Gospel are concerned with it. One might say that the feast of this day is really no more than 'a kind of renewal of the Christmas solemnity with a special reference to the Blessed Virgin' (Duchesne, *Origines du Culte Chrétien*, 1898, p. 262). Nothing could be more true.

First of all, the 'stational church' chosen for this day, as we can see in the Missal, is that of St Mary-in-Trastevere, one of the oldest of the Roman sanctuaries placed under the patronage of the Mother of God. Then, in the first Vespers of the feast, not only are the psalms those set aside for all feasts of our Lady, but exceptionally solemn antiphons, borrowed from the Greek liturgy and impregnated with a biblical savour, glorify the fecundity of the Virgin who, without the co-operation of man, brought forth the Saviour of the world. According to the first of these antiphons, *O admirabile commercium*, this wonderful interchange which was the Incarnation was brought about when the Creator of the human race, taking a body and a soul, deigned to be born of the Virgin: *Creator generis humani, animatum corpus sumens, de Virgine nasci dignatus est.* The rest of the antiphons recall several incidents of the Old Testament in which the Church has always seen prophecy of the virginal child-bearing of the Mother of God. First we have Gedeon's fleece which was mysteriously drenched with dew on a night that called forth no dew elsewhere (2nd Ant. cf. Judges 6, 36-38); then it is the burning bush that was not consumed, seen by Moses on Mount Horeb, in which we may see a symbol of the admirable virginity of our Lady which nothing can impair (3rd Ant. cf. Exod. 3, 2). In the fourth antiphon we are reminded of the stem of Jesse that brought forth the flower (Is. 11, 1), and the star that should rise out of Jacob (Num. 24, 17), both of which prefigure the virginal birth of our Saviour. Finally, in the last of these antiphons, which is indeed second to none in beauty, we hear the firm voice of John the Baptist bearing witness to him whom the Blessed Virgin Mary brought forth for the salvation of the world, 'Lo, Mary hath brought forth unto us a Saviour, whom John seeing exclaimed: Behold the Lamb of God, behold him that taketh away the sins of the world. Alleluia.' These same antiphons are used for Lauds and the second Vespers too.

Five out of the eight responses of the Roman night office for this feast sing, with discreet emotion, the ineffable mystery of the divine maternity. In the fourth of these, *Congratulamini*, it is the Blessed Virgin who herself invites us to share in her joy, that overflowing joy of the *Magnificat*:

> Rejoice with me, all you who delight in the Lord. Because I was little in the eyes of the Most High, I was pleasing to him and brought forth from my womb him who is God and man. All generations shall call me blessed, because God has looked upon his humble handmaid.

The eighth response sings of the Virgin Mother who, after she had brought forth the Saviour of all ages and the King of angels, offered him her breast full of most pure milk:

> Knowing no intercourse with man, the Virgin Mother painlessly brought forth the Saviour of the ages. None but the Virgin, whose breast heaven itself had filled, gave suck to the King of angels. The dwelling-place of a chaste womb has suddenly become the temple of God; spotless and knowing not man, she conceived a son by a word alone.

Thus we are also reminded that it was indeed at the moment when Mary pronounced her *Fiat* that, by the operation of the Holy Ghost, the Saviour was conceived.

If the chants of the Mass, except for the Alleluia, are all taken from the third Mass of Christmas, at least the prayers are different. The Collect, which will be in constant use until February 2nd, asks God that we may evermore experience the favourable intercession of her whose fruitful virginity has obtained for us the author of life, our Lord Jesus Christ; *ut ipsam pro nobis intercedere sentiamus, per quam meruimus auctorem vitae suscipere.* In the post-communion prayer, with which the celebration of the Holy Sacrifice concludes, the Church once more expresses her confidence that the intercession of the Blessed Virgin Mary will obtain for us that, by Holy Communion, we may be purified from our sins and made sharers in the grace of heavenly healing.

Finally, nothing could provide a more perfect conclusion to the Christmas octave than the antiphon of the *Magnificat* for the second Vespers of the feast:

> Great is the mystery of our inheritance: the womb of her that knew not man is become the temple of God: by taking flesh of her he was not defiled: all nations shall come and say: Glory be to thee, O Lord.'

'There is, in this praise of virginity', Dom Gajard writes, 'an impression of power, of tranquil and virile strength, which places this antiphon among the real masterpieces' (*Maria*, t. II).

CHAPTER III

THE VIRGIN MOTHER IN THE ADVENT LITURGY

THE Church desires nothing so much as to see the reign of Christ, conqueror of death and hell, fully and finally established. That is why, at the beginning of each liturgical year, during the season of Advent, she tries to direct our thoughts towards the return of Christ in glory, encouraging us to long for this and to pray for its realization. Nevertheless, because the season of Advent is a real introduction to the liturgical cycle, it prepares us to celebrate profitably all the great feasts that succeed one another in the course of the Christian year, and so, in the first place, the feast of Christmas. It naturally follows then that, given Mary's all-important part in the mystery of our Lord's birth, the Church reserves for her also a place of honour in the Advent liturgy. In fact, of course, she constantly figures in it, inseparably united to our Lord. One might almost say that from some points of view she is like a personification of Advent. It is difficult for us to imagine what must have been our Lady's feelings during the time of her expectancy, especially once she had conceived in her womb the Son whom she was to give to the world to be its Saviour. Who else, among all creatures, ever waited for, longed for, prepared for the coming of the Redeemer as did the Mother of that Redeemer? And who is better qualified than our Lady to introduce us today into the mystery of Christmas and enable us to celebrate profitably a feast which, in a certain sense, can be considered as the greatest of her own feasts?

From the beginning to the end of Advent, which in Rome

opens at the greatest of our Lady's churches in the city, St Mary Major's, by the celebration of the stational Mass on the first Sunday, the Church places us in a most special manner under the tutelage of the Virgin Mother. At the end of Compline each evening we invoke her as the 'venerable Mother of the Redeemer', *Alma Redemptoris Mater*, imploring her aid for the restoration of her people, *Succurre cadenti surgere qui curat populo*. Liturgical prayers, antiphons, responses, etc., which the Church addresses to the Virgin Mother from the beginning of Advent until Christmas are as numerous as they are moving. No less than twenty-five pieces are either directly addressed to her or mention her by name. Some of these pieces are sung many times, especially in the first and third weeks. In the first week, our Lady's part in the Incarnation is mentioned fourteen times. 'This simple fact alone', Dom Gajard writes (*Maria*, t. II), 'shows Mary's influence on the Church's devotion during these days of expectancy, all turned towards the coming Messias.' Most of these pieces bring out, with graceful and refreshing charm, our Lady's attitude of humble reserve at the moment of the Annunciation. In the history of the world, no scene has been of more capital importance, since it was precisely in virtue of Mary's acceptance of the angelic message, and the virginal conception that followed in consequence, that the new Eve controlled, so to speak, the whole mystery of our redemption with its most distant consequences. We give as an example the beautiful response *Suscipe verbum*, in which we seem to hear the human race imploring the Blessed Virgin to accept favourably the angelic message:

> Receive, O Virgin Mary, the message which the Lord sends thee through the angel: Thou shalt conceive and bear a son who will be both God and man, so that thou wilt ever be declared blessed among all women. Thou shalt bring forth a Son, but without detriment to thy virginity; thou shalt be with child but ever remaining a mother inviolate (1st Resp. for 1st and 2nd Mondays and 1st Thursday of Advent).

Have we not here the whole universe, eyes fixed on the Blessed Virgin, imploring her to express her *Fiat*, as much for her own glory as for the salvation of the world? In the third response for the first Sunday (repeated on the Thursday following), the Church represents our Lady as filled with dread because of the heavenly brightness of God's messenger: *et expavescit Virgo de lumine*. Then, taking up the words of the Angel, the Church in her turn seems to try to reassure the Virgin of Nazareth, 'Fear not, Mary, thou hast found grace with the Lord; behold thou shalt conceive and bear a Son who shall be called the Son of the Most High'.

The Approach of Christmas

In the seventh century, the Church in Spain knew only one feast of our Lady, that of her divine maternity, known simply as 'the feast of St Mary', or more simply still 'the St Mary', according to ancient Mozarabic calendars. A decree of the Council of Toledo (656), emphasizing the liturgical interest of this feast, fixed its date as December 18th, so that Christmas was always celebrated eight days after the feast of Mary Mother of God: '*Sancitur ut, ante octavam diem quo natus est Dominus, genitricis quoque ejus, dies habeatur celeberrimus et praeclarus*' (Hardouin, *Concilia*, t. III). The Church of Milan, like that of Toledo, made much of a special feast of the divine maternity which was celebrated on the Sunday before Christmas. (cf. P. Lejay, 'Ambrosien (Rit.)' in the *Dictionnaire d'archéologie chrétienne et de liturgie*, t. I, 1393).

The Church of Rome, like those of Spain and Italy, could not fail to commemorate the mystery of the virginal conception at the approach of Christmas. But she does so in a very simple and discreet manner on the Ember Wednesday of December, the day popularly known in former times as *Missus est*. The name comes, of course, from the opening words of the Gospel for that day. Certain countries, Germany, Holland, Flanders, have preserved a custom of celebrating, on Ember Wednesday, a Mass known as the 'Golden Mass', because of the special effect it is believed to have. This Mass is simply the Mass of the Annunciation celebrated with festal rite (cf. Dom Berlière, 'Le Messe d'Or', *Questions liturgiques et paroissiales*, 1920).

In the ordinary Mass for this Ember Wednesday, we hear in the Epistle the famous prophecy of Isaias, announcing that a Virgin shall conceive and give birth to a son (Is. 7, 14-15; Matt. 1, 23). In the Gospel, we witness the realization of the prophecy (Luke 1, 26-38). In those circumstances, so critical for us, it seems manifest that our Lady, because of her spotless beauty and her perfect virginity, was the only creature capable of attracting to earth the Son of God and so giving us *Emmanuel*. This explains why the liturgy of Advent and Christmas places our Lady's virginity in such evidence, setting it before us as the essential condition of her divine fecundity.

After commemorating the virginal conception, the Church proceeds, on the Friday of that same Ember week, to bring to mind modestly that mysterious scene, itself of no small importance in the work of our salvation, the Visitation. For indeed, scarcely had she conceived the Saviour of the world by the power of the Holy Ghost, than the Blessed Mother, urged by the charity of Christ acting within her, hastened— *cum festinatione*—to visit her cousin Elizabeth, so that Jesus might give himself to John. Jesus came to John borne by Mary; his action on John at this time was uniquely through her; through her he sanctified him. By making the influence of the hidden fruit of her womb felt, our Lady—the *salutifera Virgo*, as St Leo calls her—gave the world the first pledge of its redemption. At Mass on this Ember Friday, the Gospel is that of the Visitation (Luke 1, 39-47), while the Epistle, taken from Isaias (11, 1-5), tells of the stem of Jesse whence will spring the Son of Mary. At Matins, St Ambrose gives a commentary on the day's Gospel with a charm peculiarly his own. The *Benedictus* antiphon recalls the thrill of joy felt by John the Baptist in his mother's womb when the Blessed Virgin greeted Elizabeth.

Brought together thus in their proper context, the two scenes of the Annunciation and the Visitation receive from

A

the feast of Christmas, for which they immediately prepare us, new life and vigour. Moreover, thanks to the proximity of these two commemorations, we grasp more clearly the contrast that exists between two scenes that manifest, in its double aspect, the Virgin Mother's expectation. For whereas the Annunciation brings out above all the prudent reserve of the new Eve, her inviolable virginity, her obedience and simplicity, the Visitation on the other hand shows forth the merciful solicitude of the Virgin Mother, her loving eagerness to give us Christ and to be used herself for our salvation.

CHAPTER IV

THE ANNUNCIATION OF THE BLESSED VIRGIN MARY

THE FEAST OF MARCH 25TH AND THE PASCHAL MYSTERY

IN the work of mankind's redemption, the Annunciation and the Visitation are so important that, apart from their commemoration in Advent, the Church bids us celebrate each of these mysteries separately by a special feast. Nobody will complain of this. The virginal conceiving of our Lady is celebrated on March 25th, with a solemnity that would be unsuitable for the austere tone of Advent and, even more, the proximity of Christmas. Yet we must admit that the end of March is not without inconvenience as a time to celebrate the Annunciation, for the varying date of Easter obliges us frequently to transfer the feast until after Low Sunday or, at best, to celebrate it during the last days of Lent. There seems to be no doubt that in Rome March 25th was fixed for this feast before the end of the seventh century. According to the *Liber Pontificalis*, Pope Sergius (657-701) ordered a procession to be held on the four feasts of our Lady—the Purification, the Annunciation, the Assumption and the Nativity. The Gelasian and Gregorian Sacramentaries include a Mass for the Annunciation, but the feast could not have existed in the time of St Gregory the Great for he never once speaks of it. The origin of this feast, which certainly came to Rome from the East, remains obscure. Why March 25th? The popular idea is that it is reckoned from Christmas, December 25th. It seemed natural to celebrate the conception of Christ nine months before his birth. However, many liturgists hold, on the contrary, that the date of Christmas became fixed by the feast of the Annunciation. A further tradition holds that our Lord died on March 25th, and since he would have spent on earth an exact number of years, it was reckoned that the Incarnation must have taken place on the same date (cf. Dom Cabrol, 'Annonciation', in the *Dictionnaire d'archéologie et de liturgie*).

At all events, the choice of March 25th has at least the real advantage of emphasizing the Blessed Virgin Mary's part in the Paschal mystery, both as regards the Passion and the Resurrection of Christ, in becoming by her obedience the Mother of the Saviour.

This feast is as much one of our Lord as of our Lady. The Annunciation is one of those feasts on which the Church celebrates unitedly both Christ and his Blessed Mother in the realization of the same mystery, the mystery of the Incarnation considered as the starting point for the whole work of mankind's redemption. This is why many liturgical books and calendars name the feast of March 25th in a way that implies it is a feast of our Lord even more than one of our Lady: *annunciatio Christi, conceptio Christi, festum incarnationis, initium redemptionis*. But in opposition to this, the official title which this day has had for many centuries in the Roman liturgy, *Annuntiatio Beatae Mariae Virginis*, calls upon us to consider chiefly, when celebrating the mystery of the Incarnation, the part that was divinely allotted to the Virgin Mother.

Nothing brings out the fulness of the mystery of the Annunciation more perfectly than this beautiful response from the monastic Processional, which is also found in the Dominican liturgy:

This is the day which the Lord hath made: this is the day when, seeing the affliction of his people, the Lord sent them deliverance; this is the day when a woman put to flight that death which a woman had brought upon us; this is the day when God became man, remaining what he was before and taking what he had not previously. Let us therefore celebrate with all devotion the beginning of our redemption, joyfully saying, Glory be to thee, O Lord!

Two of the three prayers for the Mass of this feast express with remarkable clarity the compass of the mystery celebrated by the Church this day. First the Secret, in which, relying on our faith in the virginal conception of the Son of God made man, the Church prays that the Resurrection of our Saviour may, by his almighty power, bring us to the joys of the eternal Easter:

> Establish firmly in our minds, we pray thee, Lord, the mysteries of the true Faith, so that we who believe the Virgin's Son to be truly God and man may, through the power of his life-giving resurrection, be found worthy to attain the joys of heaven.

In its turn, the Postcommunion, praying that we may profit by the fruits of the Mass, alludes to the Incarnation of the Son of God by showing us that it is completed only in the twofold fulness of the Paschal mystery, the Passion and the Resurrection of Christ our Saviour:

> Pour forth thy grace into our hearts, we pray thee, Lord, so that we, to whom the Incarnation of Christ thy Son was made known by the angel's message, may by his passion and cross be brought to the glory of his resurrection.

Although the Blessed Virgin Mary is not mentioned by name in this last prayer, we know that it is by her having pronounced her *Fiat*, and by becoming the Mother of God's Son, that she has merited for us the work of our salvation in all its fulness. No doubt, therefore, about the importance of her intercession which demands on our part that profound faith in the divine maternity for which the Collect of the feast most fittingly prays:

> O God, who didst decree that, at the angel's message, thy Word should take flesh in the womb of the Blessed Virgin Mary, grant to us thy suppliants that we who believe her to be indeed the Mother of God may be helped by her intercession with thee.

Virgin Mother and New Eve

There could be no question as to the Epistle and Gospel for

March 25th; the choice was fixed by the nature of things. And so we find the same two readings as have already been used for the Ember Wednesday of December, the famous *Missus est*.

In the Epistle (Isaias 7, 14-15), of which the words are also found in the Communion of the Mass and the first lesson at Matins, the prophet foretells the virginal conception of the Saviour and presents it as the certain sign and pledge of our salvation:

> Behold a virgin shall conceive and bear a son, and his name shall be called Emmanuel. He shall eat butter and honey, that he may know to refuse the evil and to choose the good.

Faithful to the Gospel, traditional exegesis has always recognized in this text of Isaias a direct promise of the Incarnation, the miraculous sign foretold by the prophet being nothing else than the virginal conceiving by the Mother of God.

In the Gospel of the Mass we see the wonderful event foretold in the Epistle now actually accomplished. There can be no doubt that St Luke was told all the details of this scene by our Lady herself, and he describes it with such refreshing simplicity that it makes one of the most exquisite pages of his Gospel.

> At that time, the angel Gabriel was sent from God into a city of Galilee, called Nazareth, to a virgin espoused to a man whose name was Joseph of the house of David, and the virgin's name was Mary. And the angel being come in, said unto her: Hail, full of grace, the Lord is with thee; blessed art thou among women.[1]

When the angel came to Zachary in the temple to give him his heavenly message while he was offering incense, he did not greet him with a salutation. Similarly, when a little later an angel appeared to Joseph to tell him that his wife had conceived a son by the power of the Holy Ghost, he too was given no salutation.

But when the angel of the Lord came to Nazareth to the

---

[1] The words *Benedicta tu in mulieribus* are not in the Greek text here but are borrowed from Elizabeth's salutation.

Blessed Virgin, he greeted her with the salutation, 'Hail, thou that art full of grace!', *gratia plena*. In this phrase he revealed to her all the delight that God took in his humble handmaid. From eternity, indeed, God had chosen her among all women to be the place of his repose here below, and had jealously prepared her to become the Mother of our Saviour. At the very time when the angel came to her, Mary already surpassed in grace and in beauty all creatures in heaven and on earth. Nevertheless St Luke tells us:

> She was much perplexed at hearing him speak so, and cast about in her mind what she was to make of such a greeting.

Our Lady's anxiety was caused, not like Zachary by the sight of the angel (*Turbatus est videns*, Luke 1, 12), but by the words he spoke: *turbata est in sermone ejus*. The new Eve is the very antithesis of the old, who let herself be seduced by the deceitful promises of the serpent, and whose sin it is Mary's mission to repair. In her deep humility, the *Virgo prudentissima* shuns all praise and exaltation; hence her anxiety and reserve. She is, as it were, dazzled and blinded by the light which the angel pours into her soul, revealing to her what she herself did not see. And so, first of all, the angel has to reassure her:

> Mary, do not be afraid; thou hast found favour in the sight of God.

He then goes on with his heavenly message:

> Behold, thou shalt conceive in thy womb, and shalt bear a son, and shalt call him Jesus. He shall be great, and men will know him for the Son of the Most High: the Lord God will give him the throne of his father David, and he shall reign over the house of Jacob eternally; his kingdom shall never have an end.

It would be impossible to express the formal will of God in clearer or more precise terms. All the angel looked for was the Blessed Virgin's simple and filial acceptance of the mission he had just entrusted to her. For God never 'consults' his creature when he has made choice of one for the fulfilling of some ministry or the accomplishing of one or other of his plans. God did not ask Abraham if he minded leaving his country and his family, to go into the land of Chanaan (Gen. 12, 1-3); nor did he ask Moses if he felt up to approaching Pharaoh with a view to leading his people out of their Egyptian bondage (Exod. 3, 10). It was the same whenever God called upon some prophet to fulfil a particular mission, as we see with Jeremias (Jer. 1, 4-6) and Jonas (Jon. 1, 1-3), etc. Later on, our Lord did not consult the feelings or opinions of his disciples whom he determined to make Apostles of the Gospel. To Peter and Andrew he simply said, 'Follow me, and I will make you fishers of men' (Matt. 4, 19-22). To Matthew the publican, the two words 'Follow me' were enough. Besides, what would be the sense of refusing an appeal that one is certain comes from God? Is anything to be gained in such circumstances by 'thinking it over' or hesitating? What alternative suggestion can one make to him whose foreknowledge can never be mistaken and whose power is limitless?

Nevertheless, suddenly faced with the divine will so clearly expressed, the Blessed Virgin wonders how it can be possible for her to conceive and give birth to the future heir of David's throne, since she has vowed to have no marital intercourse with man. So we find her asking a most reasonable question of the angel Gabriel, one that in no way implies, on her part, any doubt as to the truth of the message, nor any hesitation in accomplishing the divine will.

How can that be, since I have no knowledge of man?

It is then that the angel of the Lord reveals to the new Eve the mysterious manner of her virginal conception.

The Holy Spirit will come upon thee, and the power of the Most High will overshadow thee. Thus this holy offspring of thine shall be known for the Son of God.

And he adds,

See, moreover, how it fares with thy cousin Elizabeth; she is old, yet she too has conceived a son; she who was reproached with barrenness is now in her sixth month, to prove that nothing can be impossible with God.

Unlike Zachary, Mary did not ask for a sign (Luke 1, 16),

for she had no need to be strengthened in her faith in the divine message. But the news about Elizabeth's conception filled her with the determination to visit the mother of the Precursor without delay. All that remained for her to do now as to place herself entirely at God's disposition, and this she did in those simple but pregnant words,

> Behold the handmaid of the Lord; let it be unto me according to thy word.

In that moment, the free and humble adhesion to God's will by the new Eve atoned for the sin of the first woman, whose disastrous disobedience had brought the whole human race into sin and death. Of course, in that wonderful moment, the Blessed Virgin gave no thought to the immensity of the part God had destined her to play, nor of the magnificent privileges consequent on this unique motherhood. Forgetting herself entirely, she had no desire but to serve the Lord by entire obedience in the interests of our salvation.

In speaking of Mary's 'adhesion' to God's will rather than of her 'consent' to it, the word was used advisedly. There is indeed more than a mere shade of difference in the two words, although they are used indiscriminately in common parlance. To 'consent' is really to submit to the will of another after full consideration of what is proposed or ordered. It is normally preceded by reflection varying in length according to the gravity of the matter proposed. Consent is required to conclude a pact of a contract. But it would not be correct to say that a servant consents to the orders of his master or superior. Adhesion is something more spontaneous, more complete. It does not require a judgement of the mind about some action proposed or ordered. It implies the willing engagement of the mind and heart, of the whole being. By her adhesion to God's will, making it entirely her own, the Blessed Virgin demonstrated that faith to which Elizabeth bore witness at the time of the Visitation.

No sooner had Mary pronounced her *fiat* and conceived the Word of God in her womb than the angel departed from her: *Et discessit ab illa angelus.*

Thus was brought about, in a few moments and with extreme simplicity and extraordinary suddenness, the most amazing event of the world's history, an event that had been prepared for and awaited for centuries, the Incarnation of the Son of God. The scene of the Annunciation, as described by St Luke, forcibly brings home to us the realization that if God prepares the outpourings of his grace long in advance, he wills that we should ever hold ourselves ready to respond to them with that promptitude of which the Blessed Virgin has given us so shining an example.

We are not surprised to find that on this feast of March 25th all the antiphons of Vespers and Lauds are taken from the Gospel of the day. As regards the responses at the night office, nearly all figure already in the liturgy of Advent or Christmas. They delightedly celebrate the glory that has come to the Blessed Virgin because, by her obedience, she has conceived and given birth to the Son of God. Of the eight responses of Roman Matins, it must suffice to reproduce the last, the only one that has not been previously used, *Gaude Maria Virgo*:

> Rejoice, O Virgin Mary, thou alone hast driven out all heresies; thou who didst give credence to the words of Gabriel the archangel; thou who, as Virgin, hast brought forth God and man, and, still a Virgin after thy child-bearing, dost remain ever inviolate.
>
> *V.* The archangel Gabriel, as we know, spoke to thee in the name of God; we believe that thy womb was made fruitful by the Holy Ghost; shame on the wretched Jews who pretend that Christ was born of Joseph.'

Today in the monastic antiphonary we find the original text and melody of this versicle, which elsewhere has been replaced by another.

Writing of this response in *Maria* (t. II, p. 35), Dom Gajard says that we have here 'a splendid affirmation of our Lady's virginity, both before and after the birth of our Lord, with insistence that leaves nothing to be desired; an affirmation brought out in high relief also by the soaring melody of the versicle, with its sudden burst on *erubescat*, making a sharp contrast with the more contemplative tone of the body of the response'.

CHAPTER V

THE VISITATION OF THE BLESSED VIRGIN MARY

THE BLESSED VIRGIN, BEARER OF SALVATION

WE have already seen that the Visitation is already commemorated at the approach of Christmas, but in a most discreet manner. However, such is the importance of this mystery that, like the Annunciation, it has justly become the object of a special solemnity outside the season of Advent. The feast of 'the Visitation of the Blessed Virgin Mary' was first celebrated by the Franciscan order, and only found a place in the Roman calendar in 1389, during the pontificate of Boniface IX. The feast was only raised to the rank of a Double of the Second Class by Pius IX in 1849, after his return from Gaeta. But one cannot help regretting that the date fixed for the celebration of the mystery of the Visitation should have been July 2nd, that is to say almost immediately *after* the Nativity of St John the Baptist which it ought rather to preceed and for which it should prepare.

Liturgically, the feast has nothing original about it, since, except for the two readings—the Epistle from the Canticle of Canticles (2, 8-14), and the Gospel from St Luke (1, 39-46)—the Mass is taken entirely, *mutatis mutandis*, from that of September 8th, our Lady's birthday. However, we shall do well to stop for a moment at the Gospel, of which St Ambrose gives us so valuable a commentary during the 3rd Nocturn of the night office.

The Gospel tells us that immediately after Mary had received the message of heavenly good news telling her of the divine choice of which she had been the object, she went with all speed—*cum festinatione*—to visit her cousin Elizabeth. St

28

Ambrose is careful to note that this was not because she had
the least doubt about the event of which Gabriel had told her
as a certain sign and pledge of her own conception: *non quasi
incredula de oraculo, nec quasi incerta de nuntio, nec quasi dubitans
de exemplo* (P.L. 15, 1643). Neither did the warmth of her
affection oblige her to visit Elizabeth to congratulate her on her
pregnancy and devote herself to her service.

The real motive of our Lady's action, what really produced
her intrepid resolution to span the distance between Nazareth
and Ain-Karim, without let or hindrance, was the fact that
she had conceived the Saviour and that he was anxious to
give himself to John, to give himself through his own
Mother, the Blessed Virgin Mary. 'When one is full of Jesus
Christ', Boussuet writes, 'one is at the same time full of charity,
of holy ardour, of great resolutions which lose nothing in
their execution. Mary, who bore within her both Jesus Christ
and all heavenly grace, felt drawn by a divine instinct to go
and pour forth that grace in the house of Zachary, where
John the Baptist had recently been conceived' (*Elévations sur
les mystères*). In any case it was necessary that Christ's Forerunner should be freed from all sin before being born by an
exceptional privilege, and that the Virgin Mother should
herself be the joyful instrument of this premature sanctification. Nowhere in the whole Gospel does Mary's role of
mediatrix in the work of our salvation stand out more clearly
than in the mysterious scene of the Visitation. The more so
when we remember that on this occasion John the Baptist
represented the whole human race, just as that other John, the
beloved disciple of our Lord, would represent it later at the
foot of the Cross.

Scarcely had Mary entered the house of Zachary and saluted
Elizabeth than John leaped for joy in his mother's womb:
exsultavit in gaudio. Thus the very first movement of the Precursor, when, by the instrumentality of our Lady, he came
into contact with the Son of God, was to bear witness to him,
if not by his voice, at least by a sudden thrill. Bossuet notes,
'Even a voice was not wanting to him, since it was he who

secretly enlivened that of his mother' (*ibid.*). If Jesus came to
John by his Mother, John on his side recognized him by his
own. In this way, the first witness that John bore to the
Saviour included his proclaiming, by the voice of his mother,
the holiness of the Blessed Virgin, who he saluted in these
words: 'Blessed art thou among women and blessed is the
fruit of thy womb . . . blessed art thou who hast believed'. It
is by blessing his Mother that John bears his first witness to
Christ, a witness that we repeat every time we say the angelic
salutation.

Mary's Stay with Elizabeth

Our Lady did not return to Nazareth immediately after
the sanctification of John, but stayed three months with
Elizabeth, not so much because of her close relationship with
her, St Ambrose remarks, but for the greater profit of the
Precursor: '*Non enim sola familiaritas est causa quod diu mansit,
sed etiam tanti vatis profectus*'. While John was still reposing in
his mother's womb, was it not desirable to give the unborn
Saviour all the time he needed to act upon him, to mould
him, to strengthen him in preparation for the hard lot that
God had reserved for him? St Ambrose continues in his
exquisite commentary on this part of the Gospel, 'If at the
beginning there was such an outpouring of grace that Mary's
salutation alone was enough to cause John to leap for joy in
his mother's womb and that Elizabeth herself was filled with
the Holy Ghost, we can imagine what the presence of the
Blessed Virgin must have added to this in the course of so long
a visit' (P.L. 15, 1643).

Indeed, how would it have been possible for the Virgin
Mother, inseparably united with the fruit of her womb, to
remain long months so near John without herself exercising
a deep and mysterious influence on the predestined child and,
in a certain manner, marking him with her own image and
likeness? Moreover, in such circumstances it was enough that
grace should perfect the work of nature, because, thanks to
the dispositions of God's providence, there certainly existed

between the Blessed Virgin and the Precursor a real natural affinity because of their natural relationship. It is most likely that there was, between the Virgin of virgins and him whom St Francis de Sales held to be 'more than virginal', a real likeness in temperament and doubtless a certain physical resemblance also.

Certain exegetical scholars misled by the evangelist's having spoken of our Lady's return to Nazareth before giving an account of St John the Baptist's birth, have come to the strange conclusion that the Blessed Virgin was not present at the birth of Elizabeth's son. This is to forget that St Luke is only making use, on this occasion, of a literary procedure that he frequently employs, to finish his account of one episode before beginning on another, regardless of the historical order of events. Others have even gone so far as to suggest that it was indelicate for our Lady to be present at John's birth! With R. P. Buzy (*St Jean Baptiste*, p. 42) we think that on this occasion such supposed 'delicacy' is not of any importance. Besides, does it seem likely that the Blessed Virgin Mary should leave Elizabeth at the very moment when she was about to give birth, to the great joy of all, to that son whom our Lady had specially come to sanctify and strengthen in his mother's womb by her presence? At all events, we may take it for certain that the Blessed Virgin, even more than John's parents and their relatives, was filled with joy by the birth of the child whom St Francis of Sales again calls so charmingly 'the godson of the Blessed Virgin'. This appellation, so characteristic of the Bishop of Geneva, expresses in a most delicate manner the intimate bond that united the Precursor with the Mother of the Son of God. For there can be no doubt that our Lady's long stay with her cousin Elizabeth must have created between Mary and John a real spiritual relationship of a unique kind. Does not this explain why the holiness of the Precursor bears so great a resemblance, in more ways than one, to that of the immaculate Virgin?

St John, Spiritual Son of the Blessed Virgin

The primary motive force in our profound veneration of

our Lady, the thing that draws us to her most, is surely her
extraordinary purity. She is presented to us above all as 'the
Virgin', 'the holy Virgin', 'the Virgin of virgins', 'the Queen
of virgins'. She is the personification of virginity and its
living exemplar. There is no other creature in heaven or on
earth that can even remotely attain to the purity of the Mother
of God who, from the first moment of her conception, was
full of grace. Her purity was unalloyed and knew no mingling.
Since she lived for none but the Lord, she is simplicity itself.
Her very name of Mary seems to send forth the perfume of her
exquisite virginity.

But who among men was ever more pure and chaste than
the Friend of the Bridegroom? St Peter Chrysologus declares
that from John's very birth, his holiness was a rival to that of
the angels: *nascitur major homine, par angelis* (P.L. 52, 457). St
Francis of Sales sees in him 'a heavenly man or an earthly
angel . . . an admirable human angel or an angelic man'
(*Oeuvres*, t. XVI, p. 35). Admittedly, John the Baptist was not
exempt from original sin at the time of his conception,
although this latter is presented to us in the Gospel as a very
special grace of God, the fruit of prayer, a true miracle of
which the Latin Church made mention in its martyrology on
September 24th, nine months before the feast of St John's
birth, until the fifteenth century. But at all events, it was in
virtue of a wholly exceptional privilege and thanks to the
mediation of the Blessed Virgin Mary that John was purified
and sanctified before his birth by the Saviour himself. St
Ambrose says (P.L. 15, 1644) that while he was yet enclosed
within his mother's womb, John attained the perfect age of
the fulness of Christ. In such conditions we can easily understand that, of all the saints, John alone shares with our Lady
the signal honour of being glorified in his birth.

If such was the holiness of the Precursor even before he
saw the light of day, who can calculate the degree of purity to
which he must have attained by the end of his life? He was
still in the freshness of youth when he forsook the world and
buried himself in the solitude of the desert, to receive at the

hands of God alone the perfecting of his growth. In one of his most beautiful pages, Bossuet describes him giving himself up entirely to the influence of the Word and being wholly absorbed in his greatness: 'In silence he adored him, before bearing witness to him by his words; he listened to him within, enriching himself with his fulness, before teaching men how to draw nigh to him' (*Elévations sur les mystères*).

According to St Francis de Sales, John is one of the most beautiful examples of that purity of heart that Christ insists upon so forcibly in the Gospel, and which was realized in the highest degree by the Blessed Virgin Mary. 'Lord God!' he writes to St Jane Frances Chantal. 'What wonderful purity of heart, what detachment from all things in this admirable human angel or angelic man, who seemed not to love his master so as to be able to love him more and with greater purity' (Loc. cit).

The extraordinary conditions in which John led his truly superhuman life incline one to believe that this 'admirable human angel' must have been all but wholly detached from the life of the senses. No need to recall here the tragic circumstances in which John suffered martyrdom for having stood firm as an intrepid defender of conjugal chastity in the face of an adulterous prince.

The Handmaid of the Lord and the Friend of the Bridegroom

Everything that the Gospel tells us about our Lady brings out ever more clearly her profound humility. Could there be a more striking contrast than that between the behaviour of the first woman and that of the Blessed Virgin Mary? Just as the first Eve showed herself rash and presumptuous, so did the second Eve exhibit on all occasions a most humble reserve and prudence. She is indeed the *Virgo prudentissima*, whose praises the Church never tires of singing. It is true to say that her prudence was never more apparent, never more admirable, than when she received the angelic message at the time of the Annunciation. First of all, the angel's salutation embarrassed her, because, in her humility, she wondered what could be

B

the meaning of such honours offered to so lowly a creature. But once God's will is made clear, Mary adheres to it with all her soul, proclaiming herself the handmaid of the Lord, *Ecce ancilla Domini*. Later, far from taking advantage of her glorious maternity, our Lady thinks only of serving Christ by keeping herself in the background. During our Lord's public life, when he worked his miracles and the crowds pressed round him to hear his words, the Blessed Mother discreetly kept herself out of sight. She would only appear again when the hour was come for her to join her Son on Calvary and to unite herself to him in his immolation.

St Francis de Sales has no hesitation in recognizing that the Precursor's humility was 'the most excellent and most perfect that has ever been after that of our Lord and the ever Blessed Virgin' (*Oeuvres*, t. IX). Clearly, John's most special and most noble mission made it a duty for him to draw attention to himself, since he had been sent by God to prepare the way of Christ and bear witness to the Light, *Hic venit in testimonium, ut testimonium perhiberet de lumine* (John 1, 17). Nevertheless, he makes it clear that his only intention in drawing souls to himself was so that he might lead them to Christ and give them to the Lamb of God. His whole ambition is to disappear in the shadow of our Lord. He does not wish to be taken either for the Christ, of course, nor for Elias nor for the prophet expected by the Jews. He is simply a voice, 'the voice of one crying in the wilderness: prepare ye the way of the Lord' (John 1, 23). He is the most humble servant of a Master whose shoes he declares himself unworthy to unloose (Matt. 3, 11). When Jesus appears before John on the banks of the Jordan to undergo the baptism of penance, John refuses, saying: 'I have need to be baptized by thee, and comest thou to me?' (Matt. 3, 14). The Baptist's embarrassment on that occasion is strikingly like that of his mother Elizabeth when she saw the Blessed Virgin coming to her, bearing in her womb the Saviour of the world. The more the prestige of Jesus became established, grew and spread, the more did John withdraw and efface himself. With what simplicity, a simple gesture, a single word, does he invite his own disciples to follow the Lamb of God, to whom he never ceases to bear witness. Once his mission is finished and the Master eclipses the servant, then is John's cup of joy full, *Hoc ergo gaudium meum impletum est*. His greatest happiness is to decrease as Christ increases, *Illum oportet crescere, me autem minui* (John 3, 29, 30).

Power of Mary and the Steadfastness of John

One of the many features of resemblance that one sees between the Blessed Virgin Mary and her amazing 'godson' is certainly that invincible hatred for the author of all evil which, for each of them, springs from their ardent zeal for the glory of God. Mary is the personification of gentleness, *Dulcedo nostra*. Nothing can compare to her motherly tenderness. But with the Mother of God, gentleness is not the same as flabbiness, nor tenderness as feebleness. She is the strong Virgin, and she owes her strength to the ardour of her love and her absolute virginity. No creature has a greater aversion for evil than the Mother of the Redeemer. Because of her divine maternity she is the implacable adversary of the Serpent, and it is her mission to crush his head with her virginal foot. The liturgy speaks of her as terrible as an army set in array for battle: *Terribilis ut castrorum acies ordinata* (5th antiphon of the Assumption). Bolder than Judith, more audacious than Esther, the Blessed Virgin knows neither weakness nor timidity. And nowhere does she show herself more valiant, more strong, than at the foot of the Cross. It is by a natural instinct that we call on the Mother of Christ for help and for defence against the assaults of the spirit of evil with his temptations and snares. From her also we seek strength against her enemies who are also our own, *Da mihi virtutem contra hostes tuos* (Versicle following the *Ave Regina coelorum*). The Church never tires of calling upon her to succour the wretched, help the weak, comfort those who weep, *Succurre miseris, juva pusillanimes, refove flebiles* (Ant. for Mag. II Vesp. Comm. B.M.V.). Is it not true to say that the Blessed Virgin Mary is above all the victorious Virgin in every conflict?

As we have seen, according to St Ambrose, if our Lady prolonged her stay with her cousin for several months, it was precisely with the intention of fortifying the valiant athlete that Elizabeth bore in her womb, and to infuse him with that strength which he would need in the formidable contests that he was to undergo. We may say therefore that it was thanks to the Blessed Virgin that John also was full of zeal and strength. If great delicacy was one characteristic of the Friend of the Bridegroom, great strength and unshakeable steadfastness were equally so. In many respects like the prophet Elias, whom Scripture compares to a furnace, John's soul also was an ever burning fire and his word was like a flaming torch. Our Lord himself bore witness to this: 'John was a burning and a shining light', *Ille erat lucerna ardens et lucens* (John 5, 35). There was nothing timid or mediocre about the Baptist, far from it. He had too great a love for truth and justice to be anything except intransigent where there was any question about God's rights and the purity of his worship. Herod had been guilty of adultery and put John in prison solely because he spoke out clearly about the demands of the moral law: 'It is not lawful for thee to have thy brother's wife' (Mark 6, 18). John did not hesitate to unmask the evil and to attack it at its source. We know the vehemence he used in denouncing the pride and hypocrisy of the Pharisees, that 'generation of vipers', whom he threatened with the fire of God's anger. And when the time came, the attitude of Jesus, the Son of Mary, was no different from that of his Precursor. He, also, was unsparing with the scribes and doctors of the Law, and in his zeal for the house of God he went so far as to drive out the traffickers in the temple with a whip.

Is it not reasonable to attribute the resemblance we have just noted between the holiness of the Mother of Christ and that of his Precursor to the profound influence exercised on the soul of John by the Virgin Mother during her long stay with Elizabeth? Be that as it may, we certainly honour our Lady herself when we extol the saint who was the first and most beautiful fruit of her spiritual motherhood, the saint who was proclaimed by our Lord as 'the greatest among those that are born of women', *Non surrexit inter natos mulierum major Joanne Baptista* (Matt. 11, 11). In one of his sermons (287, 1), St Augustine says, 'Admire John as much as you can; by admiring him you glorify Christ', *Mirare Joannem quantum potes, Christo proficit quod miraris*. It would be no less true to say that to exalt John is to glorify the Mother of Christ. How amply justified then is that tradition found in Christian art down to our own days of representing Christ seated on his throne of glory with his Blessed Mother Mary on his right and St John the Baptist on his left.

It is indeed surprising that at a time when there is a resurgence of liturgical, biblical and patristic studies, nothing has yet been undertaken to make better know the rôle of St John the Baptist in the work of our salvation: a rôle whose extraordinary importance seems largely to have been forgotten by the average Christian. How is it that no authorized voice is raised to recall the place of honour due in our cult to him who was the witness of the Light, the Friend of the Bridegroom, the 'godson of the Blessed Virgin', the 'greatest among those that are born of women'? Why should there be a conspiracy of silence just when John's preaching on the μετανοία or conversion of heart is so peculiarly opportune?

CHAPTER VI

THE CANTICLE OF THE VIRGIN MOTHER

THE 'MAGNIFICAT' ON THE LIPS OF OUR LADY

THE witness that John bore, through the voice of his mother, to the Blessed Virgin Mary was the sign that the secret of her glorious maternity was known. There was no longer any reason for keeping silent about the mystery that had just been accomplished in her. The hour had come for our Lady herself to reveal the wonders that God had wrought in his humble handmaid, and to give free rein to the expression of those sentiments that, until then, she had jealously guarded in the depths of her heart. Then, in singing the *Magnificat*, did she pour forth her gratitude and her joy: 'My soul doth magnify the Lord, and my spirit hath rejoiced in God my Saviour'.

No need to emphasize here the contrast between our Lady's habitual reserve and this sudden free outpouring which was Mary's reply to the congratulations of her cousin Elizabeth. Indeed, we have already noticed how, at the moment of the Annunciation, the Blessed Virgin could hardly have been more sparing of words then she was in her dialogue with the archangel. A few phrases were enough to declare to God's messenger that she was a virgin and then to express the humble adhesion to the divine will: *Ecce ancilla Domini, fiat mihi secundum verbum tuum* (Luke 1, 38). Once she had freely poured out her soul in her canticle, the Virgin Mother once again becomes silent. She said nothing of what the Holy Ghost had wrought in her even to St Joseph, the guardian of her virginity, since he only learned of it through the voice of an angel. After the Saviour's birth, the Gospel shows us our

Lady carefully marking the homage offered by the shepherds to the new-born Child and pondering their words in her heart: *Maria autem conservabat omnia verba haec, conferens in corde suo* (Luke 2, 19). All we are told of the long years passed quietly at Nazareth is the brief question our Lady asked Jesus when she found him sitting in the midst of the Doctors in the temple at Jerusalen, 'Son, why hast thou done so to us? Behold thy father and I have sought thee sorrowing' (Luke 2, 48). In the course of our Lord's public life, with the sole exception of her discreet intervention at Cana, our Lady suffers herself to be eclipsed completely, her silence is unbroken. Judging from the Gospel narrative, the Blessed Virgin seems to have uttered no word even on Calvary, in that supreme hour when the dying Christ confided her to us as our Mother.

From all that the Gospel tells us, therefore, the Blessed Mother only seems to have given free rein to her words when, in the presence of Elizabeth, she glorified God and bore witness to his power and his mercy towards Israel. Should we not learn from this, in our ordinary daily life, that if we must follow out our Lord's command in curbing those idle and useless words of which we shall have to give an account on the day of judgement (Matt. 12, 3), we need have no fear of making full use of our gift of speech when it is a matter of singing God's praises?

It may be that some people are surprised and even disappointed not to find in our Lady's canticle a more original, more personal mode of expression. Indeed, both for its background and its style, it is wholly penetrated by Holy Scripture. There is not a phrase in it that cannot be found already either in the psalms or some other part of the Bible. The similarity between the *Magnificat* and the canticle of Anna, the mother of Samuel (I Kings 2, 1-10), is particularly striking. But this absence of originality in the *Magnificat*, however much it may disconcert our modern minds, is in fact very significant. It reveals to us the state of the Virgin Mother's soul and the depth of her gratitude.

Primarily, the *Magnificat*, which poured forth from our Lady's lips spontaneously, impelled by the Spirit of Christ dwelling in her, shows us the degree to which she was herself nourished by the word of God. It is from Scripture that she draws expression for her most personal thoughts and most intimate sentiments. She makes use of the sacred writings as freely and with as much familiarity as her Son would when he made his own the sayings of the prophets and psalmists. The Blessed Virgin used the language of the Bible just like, one day, the Church would do in her liturgy. Moreover, it was because she understood the Scriptures that she was able to make use of them with such ease to express what she felt within her. There is nothing surprising in this when one realizes that, in a certain manner, the Blessed Virgin Mary was the personification of Israel, just as she would one day be the personification of that new Israel which is the Church. All that was most pure and most holy at any time in the people of God is to be found in the highest degree realized in her. Were not the noble heroines of the Old Testament foreshadowings of her greatness? Had not she more prudence than Abigail, more courage than Judith, more majesty than Esther?

In reality, if the *Magnificat* seems to us Christians of the twentieth century, the age of psychoanalysis, devoid of originality and almost impersonal, this is explained by the simple fact that the personality of the Virgin Mother, like that of Christ, is not inhibited but, on the contrary, is as comprehensive as it is possible to be; one might say it is universal. If Christ is 'the Man', as Pilate declared (John 19, 5), Mary is 'the Woman', as Jesus himself called her (John 19, 26). If Christ is the 'New Adam', Mary is the 'New Eve'. And so the *Magnificat* is, in reality, the canticle of Israel, both the old and the new, extolling the mercy of God who has faithfully accomplished his promises in the person of the Virgin Mother.

It is no exaggeration to say, therefore, that the *Magnificat* allows us to discover, at least in a certain measure, the interior dispositions of our Lady. In this canticle we can see what was the Blessed Virgin's idea of God, of his sovereign majesty, of his infinite transcendence. For the Blessed Mother, God is 'the Lord', he is 'God my Saviour', whose humble handmaid, or rather 'slave' (ἡδουλη) she proclaims herself to be, ever living in complete dependence on him who is her master. God is 'the Almighty, whose name is holy' . . . *Qui potens est et sanctum nomen ejus.* But he is also 'merciful and faithful to his promises'; *et misericordia ejus a progenie in progenies timentibus eum.*

No creature has ever possessed a greater realization of God than Mary's, that is to say, such reverential fear so praised by Scripture, and which is, even here on earth according to the psalmist, the source of real happiness: *Beatus vir qui timet Dominum* (Ps. 111, 1). Moreover, by taking flesh in his Mother's womb, Christ communicated to her the sense of the divine in a degree hitherto unknown. And having become Mother of God, far from imagining that the infinite distance separating her from the Most High had been abolished, she felt all the more her entire dependence as a creature on her Creator. Elizabeth greeted her as 'Mother of the Lord'. The Blessed Virgin describes herself to her cousin just as she had to Gabriel, when he announced her divine maternity, as 'the handmaid of the Lord', *ancilla Domini.* Such is the Blessed Virgin's humility; and, as Dom Marmion says so justly (*Christ the Ideal of the Monk*, Ch. XI), 'true humility springs fundamentally from reverence towards God', and St Teresa (*Interior Castle*, Ch. II), 'It is in contemplating his greatness that we discover our own baseness'.

Because our Lady's humility is as profound as it is true, it is devoid of all cowardliness. The Blessed Virgin is high-souled, magnanimous in the true meaning of the word. She recognizes her own greatness, being ignorant neither of the importance nor of the sublimity of her part in the work of salvation. She is fully aware of what God has already done in her and what he will accomplish later through her: *Fecit mihi magna qui potens est.* She knows what glory is reserved for the Mother of the Messias, that King whose reign will have no end. But what possesses her most, what fills her with the greatest wonder, is the work that God has himself wrought in his most humble handmaid: 'For behold from henceforth all generations shall call me blessed. Because he that is mighty hath done great things to me.' 'We have here', says Père Sertillanges (*Cahiers de la Vierge*, VIII, 1935), 'an incomparable mingling of humility, triumph, exaltation and peace. Mary is humble to such a degree that her humility becomes indistinguishable from her person, so to speak, so that God alone may triumph.'

From her humility and her mindfulness of the great things that God has done in her there wells up our Lady's gratitude, gratitude as great as the heart from which it springs. In this, the *Magnificat* is akin to the *Benedictus*. In the latter, Zachary, inspired by the Holy Ghost, gives thanks to God not so much for the personal favour bestowed upon him by the gift of a son so eagerly desired, but because of his merciful dealings with Israel: *Benedictus Dominus Deus Israël, quia visitavit et fecit redemptionem plebis suae*. If, in the *Magnificat*, Mary gives thanks to God for all his favour shown towards his handmaid, it is not so much for herself, for the personal advantages and privileges coming to her because of it, but rather because her people have become the objects of divine mercy. It is the fact of having been chosen by God himself as the instrument for the salvation of Israel that fills our Lady with joy and thrills her with happiness. For indeed, it is thanks to the Virgin Mother that the divine intervention promised to the fore-fathers of the Jewish people, to the patriarchs and prophets, has at last, after long centuries of waiting, been fulfilled. 'He hath received Israel his servant, being mindful of his mercy. As he spake to our fathers: to Abraham and to his seed for ever.'

The *Magnificat* is the reply to the divine blessing which, with the Incarnation, has come down upon all the sons of Abraham, and of which the Blessed Virgin is the particular object, solely so that she may pour it out on all generations until the end of time. Moreover, Mary gives thanks not only in the name of the ancient Israel but also of the new. From every point of view, therefore, it is becoming that the *Magnificat* should have been adopted by the Church as her own canticle of thanksgiving.

Mary's Canticle on the Lips of the Church

After the Our Father, there is no prayer so sublime as the *Magnificat*, which burst forth spontaneously from our Lady's heart once she had become Mother of God by the operation of the Holy Ghost. It is only to be expected, therefore, that a place of honour should have been reserved for this canticle in the divine office. Day by day, for countless centuries, the Church has sung the *Magnificat* at the most solemn hour of the day, that of Vespers, for which this canticle is like a tuneful culmination. The Church never allows this canticle to be omitted from Vespers even on the severest fast-days or in the office for the dead.

It is no idle question to ask what should be our own interior dispositions, we Christians, when we sing this canticle that the Church puts on our lips at the moment when she herself offers to God 'the evening sacrifice'?

The *Magnificat* burst forth from the most pure heart of Mary on the day of the Visitation with the sole intention of offering God the homage of her gratitude and her joy. It would seem most becoming, therefore, that when we in our turn give utterance to the words of this canticle, we should unite ourselves in all humility to our Lady's own thanksgiving, and thank God with her for all the privileges and blessings that she has received from the Most High. Is it not the first of our filial duties to give thanks to God for the wonders he has wrought in his own Mother, who has become our Mother too? Should we not ever rejoice with her in her blessedness and her exaltation over all creatures, especially now that she reigns at Christ's right hand in heaven, having been glorified even in her virginal flesh? For the *Magnificat* is still today, now perhaps more than ever, the perfect and always appropriate expression of our Lady's gratitude. Nothing surely, then, can give greater honour to the Virgin Mother, nothing can so touch her heart, as to hear the singing of her own canticle. Christian people make no mistake when they instinctively intone the *Magnificat* when they wish to offer God's Mother the assurance of their devotion and their gratitude.

We may add that no act of thanksgiving is more acceptable to God himself than the one that glorifies him in his Mother. What praise could more surely reach the very heart of God than thanksgiving that, in his almighty wisdom, he produced this masterpiece which reflects so faithfully his own sublime perfections? Is it not true to say that Blessed Mary, because of the wonderful resemblance between herself and her Son Jesus, discovers within herself all that there is of purity and beauty dispersed among creatures? Is she not the admiration of all the angels and saints, as the liturgy for the Assumption tells with such grace, speaking of their delight when Mary enters Paradise 'like the rising dawn, with the beauty of the moon, with the shining of the sun, terrible like an army set in array' (Antiphon for the *Benedictus*)? Is not Mary unique of all creatures to respond wholly to the plan of her Creator, and to realize perfectly the work divinely reserved for her?

But above all—and it is important to emphasize it—far from growing weaker with the passage of time and losing something of its first fragrance and force, the idea that inspired the *Magnificat* becomes daily more eloquent, more timely, given that our Lady's glory seems to blossom more and more as the centuries succeed one another. Without doubt, at the moment when Mary first sang her canticle, she had really become, by the operation of the Holy Ghost, the Mother of her Creator, and so could say in all truth: *Quia fecit mihi magna qui potens est*, 'He that is mighty hath done great things to me'. Nobody will deny that, for our Lady, the divine maternity is the fount of her most signal privileges and the point of departure for her exaltation above all creatures in heaven and on earth. However, the *Magnificat*, when it came forth from the heart and lips of the Blessed Virgin, was for a great part no more than a prophecy. It was concerned not only with the past and present but also with the future. Indeed, the divine favour just conferred upon our Lady was still far from attaining its complete development on the day of the Visitation. It was only later that the full meaning contained in advance in the words of the canticle would come to light: *Fecit mihi magna qui potens est*. What great things indeed have been wrought in her and by her since Mary first pronounced those words, in Bethlehem, in Nazareth, in the whole course of the public life of our Lord. But, above all, now that she reigns in heaven at the side of Christ, the Queen of mercy, sharing with her divine Son his universal dominion, who can recount the miracles of grace that we owe to the power of her inter-cession? How strangely modest seems to us nowadays the cultus offered by the early Church to the Mother of God, when we compare it with the devotion offered to her today all over the world, covered as it is with a multitude of sanctuaries raised up in her honour.

In spite of the divine light poured out upon her, it is certain that when Mary sang her canticle, she did not yet fully realize herself all that was contained in her own words. She could only glimpse in a far-off manner, and decidedly vaguely, the extent of the glory sent forth by her divine maternity. But now that her soul is filled with heavenly light, our Lady knows exactly the immensity of her share in the economy of our salvation. She follows its smallest developments and knows that there is no limit to the power that she can wield in our favour.

As we said just now, the *Magnificat* is today more than ever the perfect and most timely expression of that gratitude which rises from the heart of Mary towards him who covered her with blessings. The *Magnificat*, says Dom Delatte in his '*Evangile*' (Part I, Ch. 2), 'is pure worship springing from the inmost soul and mind of our Lady. All her being lies revealed in this paean of praise, as though her entire personality had become a living canticle, and must needs pour itself out in glorifying the Most High.'

It is only right, therefore, that Christian people should

unite, in a spirit of filial devotion, in re-echoing our Lady's song of thanksgiving, and that they should ceaselessly cause it to resound from one end of the world to the other, for the glory of God and the praise of his Mother. But our singing of this canticle will only be acceptable to the Blessed Mother if we are ourselves deeply penetrated with the sentiments that thrilled her own heart. *Sit in singulis Mariae anima*, said St Ambrose, *ut magnificet Dominum; sit in singulis spiritus Mariae, ut exultet in Deo.* 'Let Mary's soul be in each of us to glorify the Lord; let the spirit of Mary be in each of us so that we may delight in God our Saviour' (Commentary on St Luke, P.L. 15, 1642). But in the heart of the Mother we find the heart of her Son, and the spirit of Mary is the spirit of Jesus himself.

The Magnificat, *Canticle of the Virgin Mother and of the Church*

The *Magnificat* has to be understood like the psalms to which it is so closely akin. The psalms, which were written for Christ and are brought to their fulfilment only in him, are applied liturgically to him in person in a direct manner. They find their confirmation in one form or another in the different circumstances of his Incarnation, and they correspond to the multiple aspects of his divine holiness. However, St Augustine does not fail to remind us in his *Enarrationes* that the psalms reflect not only the experiences of our Lord personally while on earth as man, but also his experiences in the members of his Mystical Body, the Church, of which he is the head. The psalms express in turn sorrow and joy, fear, confidence, anxiety, security, through all the vicissitudes of his life's warfare.

In its own particular way, the same may be said for the *Magnificat*. It is no longer simply the canticle of the Blessed Virgin considered by herself, but the canticle of the Blessed Virgin and the whole Church. And this in no way surprises us provided we remember the close relationship that exists between the one and the other. Taken by herself, the Blessed Virgin is evidently not the whole Church, but after Christ its Head, she is its most important part. Within the mystical

Body, she holds the place of the neck that keeps the head and members together, to use an expression found in several ancient authors. Mary communicates to the Church the brilliance of her spotless purity, the sweet odour of her virginity, the fire of her charity, the price of her merits, together with all the riches of grace with which she is herself filled. No, she is not the whole Church, but alone she prevails incomparably over all the rest of the Church. Moreover, we cannot conceive of the Church without the Blessed Virgin who is, in the divine plan, its most perfect exemplar. In our eyes, Mary is like the personification of God's chosen people in so far as it represented all that was pure and holy. In a word, it is in her and by her that the junction between the old Israel and the new is achieved.

Mary personifies the Church to such an extent that the same liturgical texts are applied indiscriminately sometimes to the one and sometimes to the other. The same may be said of all those foreshadowing figures of the Church found in the Bible, which are realized first of all in the Mother of God. Mary is truly the new Eve, the Mother of the living, just as she is also, through the power of grace and the strength of her intercession, a new Judith and a new Esther. She is, no less than the Church, the Ark of the New Covenant. Almost everything that can be said of the one can be said of the other. The Church is the bride of Christ, Mary truly is also. The Church is our Mother, Mary is too, and with what close resemblance between the two forms of motherhood! The Church is the New Jerusalem, Mary is the city of God. The Church is the temple of the Most High, Mary is the true temple of the Lord, the tabernacle of the Holy Spirit: *Templum Domini, Sacrarium Spiritus Sancti* (Mag. Antiphon for Presentation of our Lady). Mary is a virgin, the Church is a virgin, holy and immaculate (Ephesians 5, 27). In a certain way the Church is modelled on Mary, just as Mary was on her own divine Son.

In the Church we see the most characteristic features of our Lady reproduced, her simplicity and her purity, her prudence and her steadfastness. Like the Mother of God, the Church is as high-minded in the service of God as she is humble and reserved in the affirmation of her privileges. Like Mary, the Church has as much tenderness and kindness for her children as she has hatred for Satan and the powers of evil. It is not surprising, therefore, that before the Church was definitely born on the day of Pentecost, she had already been represented by the Blessed Virgin in certain circumstances of our Lord's life, notably at Cana and on Calvary.

When in our turn we sing the *Magnificat*, then, let us never forget that it has become the canticle of the Church in so far as the Church identifies herself, so to speak, with the Virgin Mother, the mysteries of whose life she lives through again in her liturgy. It is a remarkable fact that there is not a word in the *Magnificat* which is inapplicable to the Church. Who, indeed, after our Lady herself, is able to magnify the Lord as the Church does in her worship that reaches the highest perfection through the inspiration of the Holy Ghost? Who can rejoice like the Church, whose songs overflow with happiness? In her own sphere, the Church can also say that 'the Lord hath looked upon the lowliness of his handmaid', for what was she before the Lord cast his merciful eyes upon her? Nothing but poor sinful humanity that Christ came to purify, to sanctify in the waters of Baptism, and make glorious by grace so as to have 'no spot nor wrinkle nor any such thing', but to be holy and immaculate, as St Paul testifies (Eph. 5, 26-27). Like Mary, the Church has every right to call herself 'blessed', she who, even in this world and in the midst of this life's warfare, shares in the triumph and glory of her heavenly Bridegroom.

It is always in his Church and through his Church that Christ shows forth the strength of his arm, doing those 'great things' of which the *Magnificat* sings. It is thanks to the Church that there came about that new order of things, foreseen by our Lady in her canticle, in which the humble are exalted and the proud are brought low. Through the driving force of the victorious Church, the Church of Pentecost, how many human powers have been subjugated or put down, how many proud schemes been broken! The triumph of the Church came about at the expense of the Synagogue which suddenly found itself despoiled of its spiritual affluence, its advantages and privileges, so that those who in their poverty hungered and thirsted for the word of God and his justice might have their fill. And how can divine mercy extend from one generation to another if not by the ever-renewed oblation offered by the Church daily on her altars, and by the power of the sacraments of which she is the sole dispenser? No need to add that it is in the Church above all that God's fidelity is manifested, since it is in her and by her that the promises passed down through the patriarchs and prophets to the true children of Abraham find their complete development and their incomparable magnificence.

The *Magnificat* is the canticle of the Blessed Virgin Mary once she had become the Mother of God. It is also the canticle of the Church and consequently of every one of her members, every Christian. All those souls who, closely embodied in Christ, share in all his states and re-live his mysteries in the liturgy, know how easy it is to find in the psalms the authentic expression of their own prayer, their supplication, their praise, their anxieties and their joys. In a certain measure, the same can be said of the *Magnificat*. It would be impossible to find a more perfect expression of the gratitude we owe to God for the wonders he has wrought in each one of us and the wealth he has heaped upon us, ever since the day when we were raised to the dignity of the children of God by our baptism.

But if the *Magnificat* is the canticle of all the children of God, it is very specially the canticle of gratitude for those who have been the objects of some privileged choice on the part of our Lord, and who are thus more closely associated with him in his redemptive work. Such are all priests and ministers of God's altar, all religious, particularly those nuns who have been consecrated as Christ's virgins and who have, for this very reason, a special right to claim as their own that canticle that came forth from the most pure heart of the Virgin of virgins.

C

The *Magnificat* is the canticle of the angels and the elect who, in the glory of heaven, unite with the Mother of the Redeemer to bless for all eternity the Father of mercies.

CHAPTER VII

THE VIRGIN MOTHER AND THE PRESENTATION OF JESUS IN THE TEMPLE

FROM CHRISTMAS TO CANDLEMAS

AFTER Christmas, while the Church brings before us the mysteries of the divine Infancy, the Blessed Virgin Mary remains always inseparable from the Saviour. On the feast of the Epiphany especially we can see the Mother of God already sharing in the royalty of her Son, seated on her lap as on a throne of glory. An unobtrusive phrase in the Gospel for this feast, which finds a place in several of the responses in the office, gives us a clue as to our Lady's part in the mystery of the adoration of the Wise Men, 'And entering the house, they found the Child with Mary his mother. And falling down they adored him' (Matt. 2, 11). In adoring the Son of Mary as their sovereign Lord, it is obvious that the Wise Men, who on this occasion represented all mankind, recognized at the same time the eminent dignity of the Blessed Virgin his Mother.

In assessing our Lady's place in the mystery of the Epiphany, we can hardly do better than quote the following reflexions of that true contemplative Cardinal de Bérulle:

'The mysteries of the Son of God must not be considered simply as actions which pass, but as ever-living sources of grace, with particular graces according to the diversity of the mysteries. We must realize that the special grace of this mystery (Epiphany) is a grace that reveals Jesus with Mary and Mary with Jesus. There are various ways of addressing ourselves to the holy Mother of God, of making contact with her, of belonging to her. There are various ways also of uniting ourselves with the Son of God. But the grace of the Epiphany is something wholly special, granting us, not to know the Son of God alone, not to unite us to the Son of God alone, but to the Son of God and his Mother both together: *Invenerunt puerum cum Maria matre ejus.* The grace of the Epiphany places them together and not one or the other separately, and we must take care to possess ourselves of the grace of this mystery with the holy kings during this octave.

'The Wise Men gazed upon Jesus and Mary at the same time; they could not see the divine Infant without seeing Mary his Mother at the same instant. One of the special honours and blessings bestowed upon the holy Mother of God is that her Son willed to manifest himself at an age and in conditions that obliged him to manifest her at the same time; for a babe can only exist by means of his mother, and is continually dependent on her to nurse and feed him. In honour, therefore, of this mystery and in imitation of these holy kings and of the King of kings, who is here wholly dependent on Mary, ever turned towards Mary, we must gather the delicious fruit of belonging specially to Mary, referring all that we have or are to her, acknowledging our need of her, our dependence on her power and her wishes.'

However, the Church feels no obligation to celebrate the mysteries of our Lord's infancy in their chronological order. Thus we find the adoration of the Wise Men celebrated nine days after the feast of the Holy Innocents, the third day after Christmas, when we are invited to follow the Virgin Mother in her flight into Egypt under the protection of St Joseph, to rescue the Infant Saviour from the cruelty of Herod. Already on the Sunday within the Christmas octave, long before the celebration of our Lord's Presentation in the Temple, we hear the aged Simeon predicting that Mary's Son would become for many 'a sign that shall be contradicted', and that she herself should feel her soul pierced by a sword of sorrow. On the Sunday within the Epiphany octave, we have barely bidden the Wise Men farewell after joining them in their adoration of Mary's Child, when the Church makes us follow in the anxious footsteps of our Lady looking for her lost Son and then finding him in the Temple at Jerusalem, sitting in the midst of the Doctors of the Law who are amazed at the wisdom of his answers. On all these various occasions our attention is naturally drawn first of all to the person of our Lord, but we always find his Mother close at hand. He still remains her humbly submissive Child, as the Gospel itself tells us expressly.

The Presentation in the Temple

This feast originated in Jerusalem, where it already existed in the fourth century. The famous Spanish pilgrim, Etheria, tells us that the Presentation was celebrated there forty days after the Epiphany, that is February 14th, with great solemnity, *cum summa laetitia ac si per pascha*. From Jerusalem the feast spread to Constantinople at the time of Justinian, under the title of Ὑπαπαντη του κυριου, 'the Meeting of the Lord' with Simeon. It does not appear to have been known in Rome before the seventh century, where it long maintained a Latinized version of its Greek name 'Ypapante'. It owes its popular modern name of Candlemas to the blessing of candles and the procession that normally precede the Mass of the day. For a long time now the calendars and liturgical books of the Roman Church have consistently called the feast of February 2nd 'The Purification of the Blessed Virgin Mary'. This title goes back at least to the Gelasian Sacramentary. But in actual fact it is not really the legal purification to which Mary humbly submitted herself forty days after the birth of her Son which is the real object of this feast. Indeed, in the Gospel for the Mass this day, St Luke emphasizes the principal end in view of our Lady and St Joseph in going to the Temple in Jerusalem: it was so that they might offer the new-born child to God his Father: *et tulerunt Jesum in Jerusalem ut sisterent eum Domino*. The object of the feast is equally demonstrated in the following *Magnificat* antiphon: 'This day the Blessed Virgin Mary presented the Child Jesus in the temple; and Simeon, full of the Holy Ghost, received him into his arms, and blessed God for ever'. A much more correct title for the feast of

February 2nd is 'The Presentation of our Lord in the Temple'.

Judging from the liturgy of the Mass alone, there is no doubt that this feast, even in the Roman Church, is primarily a feast of our Lord. The Epistle, taken from the prophet Malachy (3, 1-4), foretells the coming into the Temple of its Lord so long desired. The Gospel (Luke 2, 22-32) describes the mysterious scene in which Malachy's prophecy is realized. The words of the Introit, repeated in the Gradual, are from Psalm 47 and celebrate with religious enthusiasm thecoming of the Lord into his temple as the precious pledge of divine mercy: 'We have received thy mercy, O God, in the midst of thy temple. According to thy name, O God, so also is thy praise unto the ends of the earth.'

Finally, the Preface is that of Christmas, and of the three prayers of the Mass only the postcommunion makes any mention of the Blessed Virgin.

In the office for this feast, we find again that it is the thought of the Presentation that is predominant. This is shown by the Invitatory at Matins and the lessons with their responses. Nevertheless, texts are not wanting which bring out with great delicacy our Lady's part in this great mystery. The antiphons, psalms and versicles of the office are all from the Common for feasts of our Lady, as are also the hymns. The *Magnificat* antiphon for the first vespers gracefully draws a parallel between the attitude of the aged Simeon and that of the Virgin Mother as regards the Infant Jesus: 'The old man carried the child, but the child guided the old man. A virgin bore him, and after child-bearing remained a virgin; she adored him whom she brought forth.'

Thus, like the Annunciation, the Visitation, and above all like Christmas of which it is really an appendage, the feast of February 2nd is a feast of our Lord, but a feast of our Lord in which our Lady takes a leading part. It is natural enough that the old man Simeon, who received the Virgin Mother's Offering in his arms, should occupy a prominent place in the liturgy of February 2nd. The day has sometimes been called the 'feast of St Simeon'. Most of the antiphons at Lauds make mention of him.

On Christmas Day, the Church glorifies the Blessed Virgin giving birth to the Saviour of the world; on the feast of the Presentation she celebrates the Virgin Mother offering, publicly and as it were liturgically, the Saviour to his Father. We know that from the first moment of his Incarnation, Christ offered himself to God as the victim of our salvation, but it was necessary that he should be offered also by his Mother. He belonged to her. Our Lady had given him his flesh and his blood from her own. He was the fruit of her holiness, of her virginity, of her humility, of her obedience.

But in offering her Son, her only Son to God, the Blessed Virgin also offered herself, for never were son and mother united on earth as were the Mother of God and the Son of God. The Blessed Virgin Mary existed and lived for nobody but Jesus. When she offered in the Temple the Lamb who bore on his shoulders the burden of the world's sin, our Lady engaged herself to share in her Son's future immolation. On the same occasion also, when the old man Simeon received into his arms our Lady's precious Offering from her own hands, as though to take possession of him in the name of God and of his people, he foretold also the sword of sorrow that one day would pierce her heart.

In offering Christ to God, not only did Mary offer herself but she offered us also. In him and by him she offered us, for the Son she offered to God was offered as her 'first-born', the 'First-born of many brethren' who, by the death of her only Son, were to become her own sons. In this way, we ourselves have been brought into the Temple and have already formed, in the person of Christ, a part of that offering made by the Blessed Mother. The mystery of the Presentation is therefore a mystery that concerns each and all of us very closely. This is the mystery, in which the Blessed Virgin plays the principle part, that the Church bids us celebrate on February 2nd, and whose liturgical importance seems to be insufficiently realized these days. Let us listen to what the

Church requires us to ask in the collect for the Mass of this day, 'Almighty, everliving God, we humbly beseech thy majesty that as thy only-begotten Son, having taken flesh like ours, was bodily presented this day in the temple, so by thy doing we may be presented to thee with souls made clean' (Tr. Roman Missal, B.O.W.). Thus, on the very day (*hodierna die*) that Christ was offered in the Temple, it is becoming that we should renew in our hearts the offering made by our Lady of our own selves, in the person of Jesus, her first-born and our Chief, praying that we may one day merit in our turn to be presented in the Temple of eternal glory where Christ our Lord now resides (cf. Second prayer for the blessing of candles).

Note on the Candlemas Procession

In the preceding chapter we preferred to say nothing of the procession made on February 2nd, since by its origin it is independent of the feast of the Presentation and is not infrequently separated from it; for example, whenever Septuagesima Sunday falls on February 2nd. In this case, while the blessing of candles and the procession duly take place before the Solemn Mass on that Sunday, the feast of the Presentation is transferred to the next day. This need not surprise us when we remember that the procession on February 2nd certainly existed in Rome before the feast of the Presentation was introduced there. In spite of various hypotheses produced to account for this procession, the truth is that we do not know the reason for its introduction. There is every probability, however, that its origin was similar to that of the 'Major Litanies' which was instituted to replace a procession in honour of the god Robigus. Quite possibly, the procession of February 2nd was likewise provided to replace some similar pagan festival. Moreover, like the procession of April 25th which wound its way through the Roman *campagna*, that of February 2nd had a markedly penitential character at first, as can be seen by certain *Ordines romani* of the early middle ages. Little by little this penitential character has tended to disappear, but without doing so entirely, since the celebrant and his assistants are still obliged to take part in the procession in purple vestments.

But since for many centuries the procession of February 2nd was closely connected with the liturgy of the feast of the Presentation, it had become by the middle ages like a solemn introduction to the celebration of the Holy Sacrifice in which the Church honours the mystery of the Virgin Mother offering her only Son to God. The five prayers for the blessing of candles, which were still unknown in the ninth century, contain more than one allusion to the Presentation of of our Lord, and since the eleventh century the distribution of the blessed candles has been accompanied by the singing of the *Nunc dimittis*. During the procession which, in former days, went solemnly from the church of St Adrian to the great basilica of St Mary Major, various antiphons were sung alluding to the great mystery of the day. The most famous of these antiphons is the *Adorna*, which comes from the Greek liturgy. The Latin translation of this Byzantine trope being unfortunately incomplete and faulty, we give here a translation from the Greek which celebrates with so much poetry the Blessed Virgin carrying the King of glory in her arms:

Adorn thy nuptial chamber, O Sion, and receive Christ, thy King. Welcome with love Mary, who is the heavenly gateway; she has been made an angelic throne and carries the King of glory. The Virgin is the bright cloud, who bears in her arms her Son, brought forth before the dawn. Simeon, receiving him in his arms, proclaimed to the people that he is the Master of life and death and the Saviour of the world.

CHAPTER VIII

MARY AND THE MYSTERIES OF THE PUBLIC LIFE
OF OUR LORD

AT CANA AND ON CALVARY

IF the Blessed Virgin no longer appears at her Son's side
from February 2nd until Good Friday, it is simply because
her active and direct co-operation in the work of our
Redemption is, so to speak, suspended during the course of
our Lord's public life. In her liturgy, the Church must needs
follow what is given in the Gospel, whose discretion is
certainly not a matter of chance. Now there are only two
occasions in our Lord's public life on which the Gospel shows
us the Mother of Jesus acting in conjunction with her Son.
Nevertheless, they are both of exceptional importance, since
the first (the miracle at Cana) inaugurates our Lord's ministry,
while the second, which takes place at the foot of the Cross, is
like its definite conclusion.

Mention has already been made of the miracle at Cana on
the feast of the Epiphany in the hymns and several antiphons
belonging to that day. But it is on the second Sunday after
the Epiphany that the Church reads us, in the Gospel of the
Mass, the passage from St John which tells us of Mary's part
at the wedding in Cana. Whatever may be said about the
many and diverse explanations of this mysterious incident
that have been offered, one thing is quite certain, which is
that this miracle shows with remarkable clarity the importance
of our Lady's intercession in the work of our redemption.
There is no doubt that, at Cana, Jesus manifested his glory
for the first time, but he willed that the miracle wrought at
his Mother's suggestion should likewise manifest the power

of her intercession. It is impossible to understand the deep
significance of the miracle at Cana, or to appreciate its
importance, without considering it in conjunction with that
other scene in which the evangelist portrays the Virgin Mother
at the foot of the Cross, assisting the Saviour in filling up the
measure of his sacrifice. The miracle at Cana is the more
significant because the wine obtained by our Lady's intercession symbolizes in the eyes of the Church the Precious
Blood that our Lord poured forth on Calvary for the world's
salvation. Is there not a clear allusion to this in the Communion antiphon for this Sunday, 'thou has kept the good
wine until now'? There is no undue exaggeration, therefore,
in seeing in this miracle a genuine 'epiphany' of our Lady,
when the Blessed Virgin was manifested as the Bride of
Christ. For she is indeed united to our Saviour not only as his
Mother but also with the title of Spouse, a title that is frequently and most justly attributed to her by tradition. The
hypostatic union by which human nature was united to the
Word of God within her, already made her the Bride of
Christ, but she became even more really so in virtue of her
sharing in the Sacrifice of the Cross and the succour she gave
directly to the Saviour in the very act of our redemption. At
the wedding in Cana, in circumstances of which the smallest
details were divinely applicable to this mystery, Jesus Christ
gave us a glimpse of that union which, in his own good time,
would be achieved between himself and the Blessed Virgin
Mary, 'the woman' blessed among all others, for the salvation
of the world. The episode of the adoration of the Wise Men
invites us to honour in the Mother of Jesus, the Mother of the
King of kings; the miracle at Cana, on the other hand, reveals
to us the fact that our Lady is Spouse of the Lord of lords also
and that she shares for evermore, in heaven and on earth, his,
royalty, his power and his glory.

Apart from the incident, reported by all three synoptic
Gospels, when our Lady sought to see our Lord when he was
surrounded by a vast crowd, and being told of her presence he
compared his love for his true disciples to the love he had for

his Mother (Matt. 12, 47-50)—a passage that forms the Gospel for Ember Wednesday in Lent—we know of no other occasion when our Lady appeared during the public life of our Lord. She is next found in the Gospel for Good Friday, standing beside her Son as he finishes his mission by pouring out on the Cross that Blood that was prefigured by the miraculous wine of Cana. This was also the supreme moment when Christ, the new Adam, confided to Mary, the new Eve, his disciple John as representing all those whose own Mother she would become by the death of the Redeemer. In the Good Friday liturgy, the Church does not allow us to dwell tenderly on a scene whose touching gravity is so admirably portrayed by the sober singing of the Passion that needs no commentary.

The Feast of the Seven Sorrows

However legitimate it may be, the Church's reserve in her liturgy as regards the sufferings of the Blessed Virgin could not satisfy the piety of many of the faithful. It is not surprising therefore that towards the end of the middle ages, the more emotional trend of Catholic piety, in which the influence of St Bernard was not wanting, brought about the custom of honouring the Sorrows of the Blessed Virgin on the first Friday of Passiontide. But it was chiefly the Servites, founded in Florence in the thirteenth century, who propagated this devotion. They even obtained permission to celebrate a feast of the Seven Sorrows of our Lady on the third Sunday of September, and when this solemnity was extended to the whole Church by Pius VII, the result was a strange doubling of the feast which is quite abnormal. As Dom Capelle remarks, the text of the Mass for this feast is identical with that for the first Friday of Passiontide, except for the collect. But the offices for the two days vary, where hardly anything is the same except for the lessons from St Bernard in the second nocturn. Since the time of St Pius X, the feast of the Seven Sorrows is no longer celebrated on a Sunday but on September 15th, eight days after our Lady's nativity.

Neither the Mass nor the office of the Seven Sorrows gives that atmosphere of serenity and peace that is always found in the more ancient liturgical compositions. One has only to compare the feast of September 15th with that of the *Exaltation* of the Holy Cross, which comes the day before, to appreciate the difference. On the feast of the Holy Cross, the tone is entirely triumphant. Doubtless, taken by itself, the sequence *Stabat Mater* breathes a spirit of tender devotion towards our Lady of Sorrows; it is not without a certain lyricism, 'but how different from the lyricism of all that was handed down to us from antiquity and the early middle-ages!' (Dom Capelle). Why should the office give, for the most part, an altogether too human and too sentimental expression to our Lady's sorrow? Why represent, especially in some of the hymns, the Mother of Christ in an attitude of desolation and dejection which is certainly not in keeping with the sober and discreet Gospel story? The hymn at Matins, *Quot undis lacrymarum*, speaks of nothing but tears and sad kisses, *Sicque tota colliquescit in doloris osculis*. How different from the beautiful response, once included in the Roman liturgy and still to be found in the monastic processional, which sings of the Virgin Mother remaining strong and valiant when the Apostles fled away, and forcing herself to compensate for the failure of our Lord's disciples by her own devotion. St Ambrose tells us: 'Whereas the Apostles fled away, the Blessed Virgin stood at the foot of the Cross, lovingly contemplating her Son's wounds, for her mind was set not so much on the death of her Child as the salvation of the world' (Exp. in Luc. P.L. 15, 1930). And St Francis de Sales, with his habitual common sense, declares: 'We must notice that our Lady stood at the foot of the Cross. For some have been gravely mistaken in this matter, thinking of her as so overcome with grief that she fainted away. But this, without doubt, is wrong, for she remained firm and constant, although her affliction was greater than any woman ever before felt at the death of her son. . . . But since her love was according to the spirit, governed and guided by reason, it by no means produced inordinate emotions in the affliction that she felt. . . . Thus she remained, this most glorious Mother, firm, constant, and completely submissive to God's good pleasure, who had decreed that our Lord should lay down his life for the salvation and redemption of mankind' (Sermon for Good Friday). We should remember, then, that however grievously afflicted was the maternal heart of Mary as she beheld the cruel sufferings inflicted on her Son, she surely could have never for one moment forgotten that Christ poured out his blood on the Cross to save the world and voluntarily gave himself up to death so as to overcome death.

Easter to Pentecost

From Easter to Pentecost there is no mention of our Lady in the Gospels, neither does she find any place in this part of the liturgical year which the Church consecrates to the mysteries of our salvation. Christ was separated from his Mother when he died on the Cross. After his resurrection, he is no more of this world. If he appears to his Apostles, it is solely in order to strengthen them in their faith and teach them about the Kingdom of God. As for the Blessed Virgin, she will only be reunited with her Son on the day that she joins him in the glory of heaven. But this will in no wise hinder her from sharing to the full, more than any other creature indeed, in the joy of the resurrection. Does not the Church continually remind us of this during these fifty days by completing the office of each day in singing to the Queen of heaven the peculiarly charming antiphon *Regina coeli*, in which she asks our Lady to obtain for us that true Paschal joy which will reach its full blossoming in life eternal?

Our Lady of Joy

For a long time, down to and including today, it has pleased the faithful to meditate on and pay honour to the sorrows of the Virgin Mother. Nothing could be more reasonable, given that our Lady was so closely associated with the sufferings of her own Son. Nevertheless, it would be a

most regrettable mistake to fail to recognize the essentially
joyful character of the liturgy where it treats of our Lady. 'It
is a fact', Dom Gajard writes, 'that the liturgy in treating of
our Lady bears out most forcefully the seemingly strange
prophecy of the humble Virgin: *Ecce enim ex hoc beatam me
dicent omnes generationes, quia fecit mihi magna qui potens est*—
"for behold from henceforth all generations shall call me
blessed, for he that is mighty hath done great things to me".
Indeed our Lady's liturgy is wholly impregnated with joy.
Most of its songs of praise could be cited as bearing witness
to this, but explicit texts abound. We never tire of repeating
the pieces beginning *Beata es*, *Beata Dei Genitrix*, *Felix es*,
Gaude Maria Virgo, from her birth to her Assumption . . .
and all the "Common of our Lady" is one long cry of joy.'
Besides, what does the *Magnificat* express, as it rises daily from
the Church's lips, if not the utter gratitude and joy of our
Lady?

It is certain that in the Middle Ages there was a special cult
of the joys of the Mother of Christ. In France, churches and
sanctuaries may still be found with such names as *Notre-Dame
de Liesse*, *Notre-Dame de joye*, etc. How frequently too, in
medieval art, the Virgin Mother is portrayed as smiling as she
is glorious. The literature of those days likewise reveals the
great devotion Christians had towards her whom we invoke
as 'cause of our joy'. Several hundreds of manuscripts contain
a prayer that was to be found in most Books of Hours written
in France since the end of the fourteenth century. This prayer
refers to fifteen joys of the Blessed Virgin: the Annunciation,
the Visitation, the first movement of the divine Child, the
Nativity, the coming of the shepherds, the coming of the
Wise Men, the Presentation, the Finding in the Temple,
Cana, the multiplication of the loaves, the Crucifixion, the
Resurrection, the Ascension, Pentecost, the Assumption.
After an invocation that does not vary, 'Most sweet Lady, for
the great joy that thou didst have in . . .', the prayer sets forth
the object of joy proper to each of the mysteries of the Blessed
Virgin. The second part of the formula consists in a request

corresponding to the joy caused by Jesus to his Mother and followed by the recitation of the *Ave Maria*.

There still exists an abundance of literature from the Middle Ages on the subject of our Lady's joys: prayers, stories, poems of all sorts. The number of joys varies greatly, from 5, 7, 8, 9, 10, 12, 13, 14, 16, and even 25; which seems to show that devotion to our Lady's joys preceded that to her sorrows. In all these texts, 'It is evident', as Dom Wilmart says (*Les Méditations d'Etienne de Sallai surs les joies de la sainte Vierge*), 'that Mary is honoured, exalted, invoked, not primarily for herself, but precisely because of her most privileged and incomparable relations with the Son of God made man'.

When we realize that devotion to Mary was of such a sort, it is not surprising to find a special feast in honour of our Lady's joys celebrated in various countries, and notably in Portugal. If we see little trace of it in England or even in France, it developed considerably in Germanic lands.

PART II

FEASTS INSTITUTED IN HONOUR OF THE BLESSED VIRGIN

CHAPTER I

MARY, CONCEIVED FULL OF GRACE

WHEN the Church pays honour to the Blessed Virgin Mary, not as sharing in the mysteries of our Lord, but in those feasts more especially consecrated to her personally, the bond that unites the Mother of the Redeemer to her Son and which has won for her her most glorious privileges is always in evidence. Such is the feast of the Immaculate Conception which marks the starting point of her wonderful life, and the Assumption which was its final crowning glory.

The collect for December 8th tells us why it was that God, by the foreseen merits of the Cross (*ex morte ejusdem Filii tui praevisa*), preserved the Blessed Virgin Mary from the stain of original sin. It was that he wished to prepare for his Son, by the immaculate conception of his Mother, a dwelling place worthy to receive him, *qui per immaculatam Virignis conceptionem dignum Filio tuo habitaculum praeparasti*. For this end, it was not enough that the Mother of the Redeemer should be wholly withdrawn from the powers of darkness; it was necessary that she should be conceived full of grace and shining with heavenly beauty. It is under this positive and concrete aspect that the Gospel for December 8th explains the object of the feast. This is not the place to speak of the history of the feast of the Immaculate Conception, bound up as it is with Christian belief itself. Although the definition of the dogma took place in 1854, the actual office and Mass that we now have only date from 1863 (cf. Dom Capelle, *Questions liturgiques et paroissiales*, Avent 1954). Fixed for December 8th, exactly nine months before our Lady's nativity (September 8th), the feast of the Immaculate Conception always falls at the beginning of Advent. The Gospel for the feast is very brief, no more than three verses of St Luke's account of the Annunciation, stopping short expressly with the end of the archangel Gabriel's salutation of our Lady, before revealing to her the purpose for which she had been chosen by God: *Ave gratia plena, Dominus tecum, benedicta tu in mulieribus*. In this solemnity the Church does not consider the Blessed Virgin solely as having been exempted from the stain of original sin, but honours her chiefly because of that plenitude of grace given her by God from the first moment of her existence in view of her future maternity. The feast of December 8th sets before us the Mother of the Saviour already shining in her conception with such great beauty that the whole universe breaks into the cry of wonder and praise: *Tota pulchra es, Maria, et macula originalis non est in te*, 'Thou art all fair, O Mary, and the stain original was never in thee' (1st Antiphon for Vespers and Lauds, and versicle for Alleluia). Indeed, the whole liturgy for December 8th, that of the Mass above all, is redolent of the Blessed Virgin contemplated in her fulness of grace and the blossoming of her supernatural splendour. In the Offertory antiphon, the Church takes up again the last words of the Gospel to salute, in her turn, the Immaculate Virgin and proclaim her *gratia plena*.

The Mass Gaudens gaudebo

The fundamental attitude of the Church in the cult she offers to our Lady is, without any doubt, one of selfless love and praise. Naturally this praise ever rises, as it must, to God himself, the author of all those wonders accomplished in the Virgin Mother. Nowhere is this more so than in the liturgy of December 8th, for among the mysteries of the Blessed Virgin, none so clearly manifests the gratuitousness of the divine predilection for our Lady as does her immaculate conception. No wonder then that all the chants of the Mass for this feast give thanks to God, in one form or another, for the realization of that plan which he had himself conceived before the creation of the world. This is recalled in the passage from the book of Proverbs that the Church has chosen for the Epistle, putting the words on the lips of the Immaculate Virgin.

If we are going to thank God for the masterpiece he has achieved in the person of the Virgin Mother for the glory of his own Son who is also hers, we must first of all and above all do as the Church does in the introit *Gaudens gaudebo*, unite ourselves to the praise offered by our Lady herself in proclaiming her gratitude and her joy for having received from her Creator all that beauty with which he sees her clothed:

> Joyfully will I rejoice in the Lord, and my heart shall triumph in my God; for he hath clothed me in the garment of salvation, his mercy enfolds me like a cloak, as a bride adorned with her jewels (Isaias 61, 10).

Of course, in this beautiful text from Isaias, we hear Jerusalem expressing her gratitude to God for the restoration she will enjoy in the Messianic age. But, making use of her lawful rights, the Church here appropriates the words of the prophet to make them well up from the heart of our Lady. In this antiphon, so suggestive of the tone of the *Magnificat*, the Blessed Virgin sings her joyful gratitude to him who, from her very conception, not only preserved her from the stain of original sin, but filled her with the riches of his grace to an extent no other creature had ever known.

The other liturgical texts of this Mass, while paying direct homage to our Lady, ascend likewise to God, as to the author of the wonders wrought in the Mother of his only Son. We see this clearly in the Gradual-response, where the Church delights to put on our lips those praises which the leaders and the people of Israel offered Judith after her victory over Holofernes:

> Blessed art thou, O Virgin Mary, by the Lord the Most High God, above all women upon the earth (Judith 13, 23).

Such praise is indeed far more appropriate for that woman,

blessed among all others, of whom Judith was no more than a
humble figure, Mary, who, by the grace of her conception,
gained that first and decisive victory over the serpent, which
the liturgy of this feast celebrates so assiduously. (cf. The
antiphons of the *Benedictus* at Lauds, that of the *Magnificat* at
2nd Vespers, and several versicles and responses.)

The Communion antiphon provides us with a final salutation for the Immaculate Virgin, offering up to God all those
praises directed to her in the course of the Holy Sacrifice:

> Wondrous things have been said of thee, O Mary, for
> he that is mighty hath done great things to thee.

The first part of this antiphon is taken from Psalm 86.
Fundamenta ejus. The Church justly applies to our Lady what
the psalmist says of the city of God, Jerusalem. This part of the
antiphon alludes to all those praises offered to the Blessed
Virgin during the Mass just celebrated. Cleverly joined to this
fragment from the psalm we have, in the second part of this
antiphon, another text of Holy Scripture, a verse of the
Magnificat, in which the Blessed Virgin hersalf pays homage to
the divine omnipotence for all that he has deigned to accomplish in his humble handmaid.

Since the Mass for December 8th is offered, with all
befitting solemnity, in honour of the Immaculate Conception,
it is only natural that the Church should plead on our behalf
for the grace more specially connected with the mystery
celebrated. And what more apposite gift could she ask, by the
intercession of the spotless Virgin, than that of purity of soul
and body? This, then, is the grace for which we ask in each of
the Mass prayers, but more especially in the Collect which is
used also at each 'hour' of the divine office.

> O God, who by means of the Immaculate Conception of
> the Virgin didst prepare a worthy dwelling for thy Son,
> and foreseeing his death, didst thereby preserve her from
> all stain, grant that we too by her intercession may come
> to thee unstained by sin.

With gratitude and joy as the predominant features of this
feast of the Immaculate Conception, we may hope for a share,

in a certain manner, in the signal privilege of the Mother of Christ (who is our Mother also), by obtaining a more complete cure of those wounds which are the inevitable consequence of our sins. The postcommunion prayer sums up in precise terms what should be the fruit of our Communion in the Sacrifice of this feast:

O Lord our God, let the sacrament of which we have partaken heal in us the wounds of that sin from which the Conception of Blessed Mary, and of her alone was by thee kept immaculate.

CHAPTER II

OUR LADY'S EASTER

DIGNITY OF THE FEAST OF AUGUST 15TH

THE greatest of our Lady's feasts, the Assumption, celebrates the Blessed Virgin's own special share in the triumph of her Son over sin and death. The solemnity of the Assumption originated in the East where it already existed in the sixth century, as we know from the fact that the Emperor Maurice (†602) gave orders that it should be celebrated on August 15th throughout the Empire. From this we may deduce that its actual institution must go back at least to the beginning of the sixth century. Dom Cabrol (*Assomption* in the *Dictionnaire d'archéologie et de liturgie*) suggests that the feast probably took its rise at the tomb of the Blessed Virgin, prompted by the pilgrimages made to this spot. It came to Rome in the first half of the seventh century. Its first appearance in writing is in the Wurzburg book of the Gospels, which makes no mention either of the Annunciation or our Lady's Nativity, but calls the Assumption the *Natale*, thus considering it the principal feast of our Lady. From the fact that the Assumption is the indispensable complement of the Paschal solemnity, it is, among all the saints' days of the year, the one most closely associated with the Proper of the Season, that essential part of the liturgical cycle in which we revive annually the work of our salvation in its full development.

For indeed, all is not over when we have watched Christ ascend into heaven, there to sit at the right hand of God and, as the Great High Priest, bestow upon us the fruits of his own sacrifice. The cycle of our redemption must not be considered as having completed its orbit until we reach that glorious day on which we see the new Eve reunited with the new Adam in heaven, there to share with him the honours of a victory of which she was the instrument chosen by God. For, in conformity with a disposition of divine providence whose befittingness is extolled by the Fathers of the Church, the amplitude of the reparation had to surpass the extent of the damage caused by the Fall, so that Christ must necessarily be united with his Spouse, the Blessed Virgin, in the same work and in the same triumph, so as to give back life to all those who had been dragged down to death by our first parents' sin.

The importance of what was achieved in the person of the new Adam, become the author of life by reason of his sacrifice, is of such a nature that the Church reckons it her indispensable duty to lead us by successive stages through all the parts of the work of our salvation, Incarnation, Passion, Burial, Resurrection and Ascension, which are all united in the one Paschal mystery by which Jesus Christ enables us to pass, with him and in him, from this world to the Kingdom of his Father. As for our Lady's passage thence, we celebrate it in a single feast, but one that is the more glorious and the dearer to Christian piety in that it sums up for us all the mystery of her sublime Assumption. A monk of the eleventh century, John Mauropos, bishop of Euchaita, defined the object of this most beautiful, most comprehensive of our Lady's feasts as follows: 'Today we celebrate the falling asleep of the Mother of God, the burial of the Mother of God, the resurrection, the ascension, the exaltation of the Mother of God; marvel added to marvel, one after another, for this Mother of God is the Daughter of God, the Spouse of God; and this Spouse is ever a virgin, this Queen seeks above all to be a handmaid' (P.G., 120, 1080).

The wonderful complexity of this feast of August 15th accounts for the fact that it goes by many different names in ancient liturgical books, each of which happily brings out some fresh aspect of this mystery of the Blessed Virgin. The terms *Dormitio* (κοίμησις) or *Pausatio* tell of the sweetness of a death brought about, as was said, by an excess of love (cf. St Francis de Sales' *Treatise on the Love of God*, and Bossuet's Sermons on the Assumption). The term *Natale* well becomes this greatest of our Lady's feasts by corresponding with her resurrection, just as her Son's Resurrection has the character of a birth, that of his human body into the life of heaven. As regards the title Assumption, found in the Gelasian and Gregorian Sacramentaries, it was only to be expected that it would prevail over the other names, because, taken in its widest meaning, it not only signifies the fact, now defined by the Church as divinely revealed, of the bodily ascension of our Lady, but it also recalls the whole mystery of the sublime exaltation of the humble handmaid of the Lord, whom God was pleased to raise up to heaven, there to reign at her only Son's right hand.

With intent to show the great difference between our Lord's exaltation to heaven and that of the Virgin Mother, the Church in her liturgy reserves the word '*Ascension*' for the triumph of Jesus Christ rising up to heaven by the power of his own divine nature. For the triumph of our Lady, the word '*Assumption*' is used, to indicate the fact that the Blessed Virgin Mary owes her exaltation to the power of her own Saviour. *Ascension* comes from *ascendera*, meaning 'to rise up'; whereas *Assumption* comes from *adsumere*, meaning 'to take to oneself'. When referring to our Lord's Ascension, the Mozarabic, Gallican and Ambrosian liturgies use the word *Ascensio*; in the ancient Roman Sacramentaries, one finds *Ascensa*.

The Falling Asleep of the Mother of God

We have already quoted the expression of John Mauropos: 'Today we celebrate the falling asleep of the Mother of God, the burial of the Mother of God . . . '. Since the Roman Church received the feast of August 15th in the form used already in the Eastern Church whence it came, there can be no doubt that the solemnity celebrated was not the immortality of the Blessed Virgin, as some modern writers have supposed, but her death and her resurrection. Dom Capelle, whose competence nobody will question, has proved this in a way that seems to us unanswerable. Moreover, in the Secret prayer of the Mass in use until 1950, that is to say until the definition of the dogma, the Roman Church openly expressed her belief in the death and the resurrection of the Blessed Virgin by the words: 'Let the prayers of the Mother of God come to the aid of thy people, O Lord. We know that, as is the lot of all mankind, even she has passed away from among us; nevertheless, make us to feel that in thy glorious heaven, she is for evermore our advocate with thee; *quam pro conditione carnis migrasse cognoscimus*'.

Never was the object of the feast of August 15th as celebrated by the Roman Church better defined liturgically than in the ancient prayer *Veneranda nobis*, found in the Gregorian Sacramentary sent to Charlemagne by Pope Hadrian I (772-795). Composed by order of Pope Sergius I towards the end of the seventh century, this prayer is very nearly contemporaneous with the introduction of the feast in Rome. It used to be sung at the start of the procession which, on August 15th, made its way to St Mary Major's basilica where the solemn Mass took place. For several centuries this prayer *Veneranda nobis* had its place in the Roman liturgy. Today it is still to be found in the Dominican liturgy and certain other local ones. Here, then, is its text, whose doctrinal importance has no need to be underlined and which not a few people regret was not included in the new Mass of 1950:

> Most worthy of our veneration, O Lord, is the feast of this day on which the holy Mother of God underwent temporary death (*mortem subiit temporalem*), but could not be held captive by its bonds (*nec tamen mortis nexibus deprimi potuit*), she in whom thine only Son our Lord took human flesh.

This text leaves no shadow of doubt about the fact that the feast of the Assumption as celebrated by the Roman Church had, for its object, both the death of the Virgin Mother as one subject to human conditions and her resurrection as a necessary consequence of her divine maternity: *quae Filium tuum Dominum nostrum de se genuit incarnatum.*

There is no reason then to restrict nowadays the object of the feast of August 15th, and to exclude from its solemnity— as some theologians would like to do—the celebration of the death of the Blessed Virgin Mary which, until 1950, was openly and constantly affirmed by the Roman Church in her liturgy. 'By what strange mysticism', writes Dom Capelle, 'would one wish that she who as *socia Christi* was so utterly ours, body and soul, should not have been so *usque ad mortem*?' The omission of the prayer *Veneranda nobis* from the new form of office and Mass introduced after the definition of the dogma in 1950, is perhaps explained by the fact that the prayer clearly speaks of the death of the Blessed Virgin, but the Holy See did not wish this to be implicitly judged to be included in the definition. This accidental circumstance should not hide from our eyes the unanswerable witness given by the prayer in question. At a time (end of the seventh century) when the bodily Assumption was by no means accepted everywhere, the premier Church in the world placed this clear formula in her liturgy and maintained it until the thirteenth century (*Ephemerides liturgicae*, 1952, p. 241). How correct, therefore, is the conclusion of an article in the *Nouvelle revue théologique* (December 1954), in which R. P. Galot writes: 'After Christ and with him, Mary passed by death so as to have the victory over it. It was a passing to the splendour of the Assumption. Is it not consoling to us to know that the Mother of God has known death before us? Has she not made death more familiar, more worthy of honour, for us? And above all, by transforming death into a victory, does she not encourage us in our hopes for the life hereafter? When we carefully think over the subject surely we see that there is nothing more eloquent than the simple and obscure death of Mary, and that a most important feature in her life and in ours would be missing if this death had not taken place.' This seems to be the language of common sense.

The Assumption of the Blessed Virgin, Bride and Queen

After celebrating the triumph of Christ our Head in the course of the Paschal solemnity, the Church celebrates that of Mary on August 15th. This feast is the more dear to Christian piety in so far as the Assumption of Mary is, in the last resort, no more than the necessary complement to the exaltation of her Son, as we sing in that beautiful antiphon *Ascendit Christus*, still preserved in the monastic processional. It is only right, therefore, after celebrating our Lord's Easter, to celebrate that of our Lady. In the old Mass of the Assumption, this thought was forcefully brought out in the joyous Introit *Gaudeamus*, which invited us to extol the Virgin Mother for her glorious Assumption in which the angels rejoice and praise the Son of God, *In cujus Assumptione gaudent angeli et collaudant Filium Dei*. Many liturgical texts, happily reproduced in the more recent office, show us the Virgin Mother rising above angelic choirs which joyfully sing of this new victory of their own Lord: *Assumpta est Maria in coelum, gaudent angeli, laudantes benedicunt Dominum*—'Mary is taken up into heaven, the angels rejoice and bless the Lord with praise' (1st Antiphon for Vespers, etc.).

We cannot think of the Son of Man throned in heaven in the fulness of glory without having near him that woman, blessed above all others, who, both as Mother and as Bride, had so intimate a part in the establishment of his kingdom. It is the joyful day of the Assumption also that witnesses the achievement of that union between the new Adam and the new Eve, whose magnificence had been prepared by divine Wisdom from the beginning. Nothing is now wanting for the celebration of the royal marriage, once the blessed Virgin Mary has risen to heaven and reigns there with Christ, as the antiphon for the *Magnificat* proclaims: *Hodie Maria Virgo coelos ascendit, gaudete quia cum Christo regnat in aeternum*. For in the feast of the Assumption, the object of the Church's celebration is the glory of the Virgin Mother rejoining her Son in heaven to take her place at his right hand and reign with him eternally (cf. Invitatory at Matins, 2nd Ant. for Vespers, etc.). The

universal royalty that Christ already possessed in his capacity
as only Son of God, he merited anew, by his Cross, not only
for himself but also for the woman who had been the
indispensable instrument, the faithful and most willing
collaborator in his victory over the powers of evil. As Pope
Pius XII expressed it in the encyclical *Ad coeli Reginam*, 'As
Christ, the new Adam, is our King because he is not only
Son of God but also our Redeemer, it is equally lawful to
affirm that, by a certain analogy, the Blessed Virgin is queen,
both because she is Mother of God and also because, as the
new Eve, she was associated with the new Adam'.

As Christ became 'Lord' on the day of his glorious exaltation, so in her turn the Virgin Mother became, on the day of
her Assumption and her crowning, 'our Lady'. No wonder
that this appellation has ever been dear to Christians, since we
cannot use it without at the same time recognizing, with most
filial devotion, our entire dependence here below on her who
is Queen of heaven and earth. St Stephen, King of Hungary,
was wisely inspired to proclaim that in his kingdom August
15th was *Dies magnae Dominae*, the day of the great Queen.

The liturgy of the Assumption, moreover, describes our
Lady's entry into heaven as that of a majestic queen whose
coming, long awaited and desired by angels and saints, stirs
up a thrill of enthusiastic joy. Where could we find this more
exquisitely expressed than in the *Benedictus* antiphon which
sings so gracefully of the delight of the heavenly court when
the Virgin Mother enters the palace of the King 'splendid as
the dawn, beautiful as the moon, shining like the sun, terrible
as an army set in array for battle'? No less charming is the
antiphon *Virgo prudentissima*, in which we seem to hear those
who still dwell on earth salute in their turn, but with a tinge
of regret, the departure from among them of the loveliest of
God's creatures, 'Virgin most prudent, whither goest thou,
like to the rosy dawn? Daughter of Sion, all beautiful and
sweet art thou, fair as the moon, chosen as the sun.' And
although it has its place in all feasts of our Lady, nowhere
does the psalm *Eructavit cor meum* (Ps. 44) appear so rich in

light and poetry as on this day of the Assumption, when the Blessed Virgin rises up to heaven clothed in glory to take her place at the right hand of her Bridegroom, the King of kings, *Adstitit regina a dextris in vestitu deaurato, circumdata varietate.* No excuse need be made to justify the many liturgical texts borrowed from this royal nuptial poem which sings so magnificently of the union of Christ and his Bride, the Blessed Virgin Mary.

As far as we are concerned, it is clear that the cycle of the mysteries of our redemption is only finally complete on that day when the Mother of God, glorified even in her virginal flesh, begins to reign in heaven. The Sacrifice of the Cross was finished and the Sacred Victim accepted; the Saviour, risen again to his Father's right hand, had become himself the source of our life. One thing more was needed: it was necessary that the Blessed Virgin, Bride and Mother of the Redeemer, should intervene on our behalf in pouring out the riches bought on Calvary. Hers it is to know, in the light of glory, the prayers and needs of her children and to pour out on each of them the vivifying waters of the grace of Christ. Is it not for the new Eve to offer the fruit of life, just as the former Eve gave us, through Adam, the fruit of death?

The Virgin Mary, Bride of Christ

The title, Bride of Christ, *Sponsa Christi*, is nowadays so constantly applied to our Lady that one hardly considers it necessary to justify its use. Obviously the title of Bride or Spouse does not apply to the Blessed Virgin in the sense of the word as ordinarily used, but it is perfectly legitimate to use it for her by analogy, and an analogy that is well founded.

In the Eastern Church from the fourth century, there was no hesitation in following St Ephrem in calling Mary the Spouse of Christ. The Western Church, with its habitual reserve, waited until the eighth century before attributing this title to the Mother of God. It is true to say that even today texts in which the Blessed Virgin Mary is spoken of formally as the 'Bride of Christ' are still very rare in the

Roman liturgy. It is easy to understand this reserve. Neverthe-less, since this title is commonly given to the Church both by Holy Scripture and the liturgy, it appears to be perfectly legitimate to apply it also to the Blessed Virgin, who is held to be the type, even the personification of the Church by Christian tradition. We might add that if the Church herself in her liturgy does not hesitate to recognize in the numerous virgins whose memory she honours true brides of Christ, because of their intimate union with him whose divine beauty attracted them to leave all else for him alone, how can we fail to recognize the Immaculate Virgin as the perfect Spouse of the Word made flesh? *Si enim virgines sponsae sunt Agni, quomodo non virgo virginum sponsa sponsarum?* (Richard of St Laurence, *De laudibus*, I, 54). In a sermon attributed to St Albert the Great, the author says: *Dicitur enim sponsa (Virgo Maria) propter inaestimabilem charitatem qua reciproce se diligunt Mater et Filius*, 'Mary is called spouse because of the incal-culable love which Mother and Son have for one another'. And R. P. Barré, in *Etudes Mariales* (1951), says that this association of love only reaches its fulness in glory, as well for the Church as for Mary. On the day of the Assumption, the Blessed Virgin is brought into the presence of the Sovereign Lord of all, so that even before the definition of her bodily glorification, Ambrose Autpert could address these words to her: *Teque ipse Rex regum et matrem veram et decoram sponsam amoris amplexu sibi associat.*

Mary's claim to the title of Spouse in a sense that is hers alone arises from the fact that it was in her and by her that the union between the Son of God and human nature was effected. In becoming man, the Word espoused the whole of human nature in that individual nature that he took personally. 'God the Father', says St Gregory, 'made a marriage for his Son when he united him to human nature in the Virgin's womb' (Homily, 19th Sunday after Pent.).

But we must also consider the very special character of our Lady's maternity. 'There is a generation that is different from all others. Where can we find the son who chose his own mother and asked her consent like the bridegroom asks the bride's? What son is there who created the mother of his choice: *genuisti enim qui te fecit*? Where is the son who freely, by a sort of spontaneous creation of his love, took flesh in his mother? Who is the son who sanctifies his mother and gives himself to her as her Saviour, her salvation, her perfection, the model she must follow in seeking that perfection? It is the mother's lot to give her child birth and then to accept all the heart-rending separations that successively follow one another until the child, having grown up, finally leaves home to make his own life. Mary's lot is to enter day by day into the mystery of her Son until that day when Jesus himself will take her to himself, to crown her at his Father's right hand.' (A.-M. Henry, o.p., *La Vie Spirituelle*, May 1949, p. 467.)

The Virgin Mother's work is not over with the mysteries of Christ's infancy. If she effaces herself during our Lord's public ministry, we find her again at the foot of the Cross, uniting herself to the immolation of her Son. It is there that she co-operates directly in the birth of a new humanity, like the new Eve at the side of the new Adam. She is truly for Christ what the first woman was for the first man, an aid like to himself, *adjutorium simile sibi*.

Finally, if it is true that the title Mother of God is the one most suitable for the Blessed Virgin Mary, and consequently her most striking claim to glory, it is no less true that the title of Spouse given to our Lady has the advantage of bringing out the ineffable bond of love that the special circumstances of the Incarnation created between the Mother and the Son.

It is wholly legitimate therefore to give the title of Spouse of Christ to the Blessed Virgin Mary, but by no means that of Spouse of the Holy Ghost, as certain authors have done. The title of spouse, like those of husband and wife, can be applied only to beings possessing, according to the diversity of sex, the same human nature.

E

CHAPTER III

CHRISTMAS IN THE AUTUMN

THE NATIVITY OF THE VIRGIN MOTHER

ON September 8th, the Church celebrates the birth of the Blessed Virgin Mary. This day has not normally the solemnity and the grandeur of the Assumption, in which the liturgy celebrates magnificently the glory of our Lady seated in the heights of heaven. But the feast of September 8th owes its own particular charm to the intimacy and exquisite freshness that belongs to it. It is like Christmas in the autumn, and in our calendar our Lady's nativity has a peculiarly appropriate place, since it is celebrated at the beginning of a season in which nature seems to grow calm after the burning heat of summer, and to rest awhile before having to face the rigour of winter. The sun's rays are no longer blinding in their brilliance, but seem rather to spread over all creation a light whose gentleness is unequalled. No time of year is so suitable as the beginning of autumn for celebrating the Blessed Virgin in the most peaceful, the most silent and, in a certain sense, the most joyful of her mysteries.

The Church of Jerusalem was the first to honour the memory of our Lady's nativity on September 8th in a basilica situated near the Probatic Pool, on the site of a house which tradition said was that in which Mary was born. In Rome, the feast was still unknown at the time of St Gregory the Great. But it had certainly been adopted by the end of the seventh century, for it is mentioned in the *Liber pontificalis* of Pope Sergius I (687-701). It was this pontiff who decreed that on the four feasts of our Lady, of which her nativity was one, a procession should go from the church of St Adrian to St Mary Major's.

From then on, the feast spread rapidly all over the West, especially in France. In the eleventh century, St Fulbert, Bishop of Chartres, lent considerable weight to its diffusion, as can be recognized in his city to this day.

This feast is surely among the most joyful solemnities of the liturgical year. In the antiphons and responses of the office, the Church constantly exhorts us to celebrate the birth of Blessed Mary with joy: *cum jucunditate nativitatem beatae Mariae celebremus* (1st Ant. for Vespers, 1st and 2nd Response for Matins, etc.). This joy, it is true, is a joy that is intimate and very tender, the joy of dawn. As St John Damascene (P.G. 96, 662) declares, 'it is most becoming to celebrate joyfully the natal day of the world's joy'. St Peter Damian, in an enthusiastic sermon for September 8th (P.L. 144, 741), says that the whole Church rightly celebrates, *profusis gaudiis*, the birthday of the Mother of the Bridegroom. 'Let us rejoice', he says, 'in this day on which we celebrate, with the birth of the Blessed Virgin, the beginning of all Christian festivals.'

The Gospel of the Mass reminds us (Matt. 1, 1-16) that it was on the day that the Blessed Virgin was born into the world to give it the Saviour so long awaited, that the promise made by God himself to Abraham and again to David was finally realized. Besides, by applying the passage from the book of Proverbs (Prov. 8, 22-35), read as the epistle, to the Blessed Virgin, the Church gives us to understand that, in the divine mind, the Son of the Virgin was as inseparable from his Mother as the flower is from its stem from the very dawn of creation.

At all events, as we find so charmingly expressed in the response *Solem justitiae*, the Virgin Mother, Star of the sea, only appeared in this world in order to give birth to the Sun of justice, our Sovereign King: *Solem justitiae, regem paritura supremum; stella Maria maris hodie processit ad ortum*. Another response, still preserved in the monastic responsorial, sings of Mary as the delicate stem which is only detached from the root of Jesse in order to bring forth a flower on which the Spirit of God reposes: *Stirps Jesse virgam produxit, virgaque florem, et super hunc florem requiescit Spiritus almus.* It is becoming, therefore, that on the very day on which we celebrate the Blessed Virgin's birth, the Church already pays honour to her future maternity. There is, in fact, not a single chant of those in the Mass for September 8th that does not speak of her divine maternity. Nothing brings out the significance of this feast better than this antiphon of Greek origin which brings the feast to a close: 'Thy birth, O Virgin Mother of God, was a token of joy for the whole world, for it was of thee that was born the Sun of Justice, Christ our God, who, destroying the curse, poured forth a blessing and, confounding death, granted us life eternal' (*Magnificat*, 2nd Vespers). Mary only came into the world, therefore, to give human life to him who, by his human death, has given us his own life, the life of eternity. Before giving himself to us, the Saviour of the world chose to give us his Mother, so that he might give himself to us through her.

When Christ's forerunner was born in those wonderful circumstances of which the Gospel tells us, the event was welcomed with immense joy not only by Elizabeth's kinsmen, but by the whole neighbourhood, for it was clear to everybody that some special destiny was reserved for this child on whom the Lord had laid his hand: *Etenim manus Domini erat in illo* (Luke 1, 66). When our Lady was born, nobody could have guessed the great things that God had determined to do through this child who would one day be enthroned in heaven at the right hand of his only Son. We are not surprised, then, that the birth of the Mother of God, in circumstances of which we know nothing, was as humble and hidden as would later be that of our Saviour. But today, while on September 8th we commemorate our Lady's nativity, we cannot forbear to think also of that other birth, soon to bring peace and joy to the whole world. In the Collect for the Mass on September 8th, the Church asks for an increase of peace, and this is obviously the peace to men of good will that our Saviour brought to us on Christmas night. But the Virgin Mother can only cause genuine peace, the peace of Christ, to grow

within us by the constant exercise of her spiritual maternity.
After having brought forth Christ in human flesh to give him
to the world, our Lady continues by her powerful intercession and her merits to bring forth in souls the ever growing
influence of him who is, in St Paul's words, our peace: *Ipse
enim est Pax nostra* (Eph. 2, 14).

'And the Virgin's Name was Mary' (Luke 1, 27)

Within a few days of Christmas the Church celebrates the
holy Name of Jesus, and so, in like manner, on September
12th, a few days after our Lady's birthday, comes the solemnity of the holy name of Mary. This feast, originally granted
by Pope Julius II to some Spanish diocese, was extended to
the whole Church by Innocent XI in memory of the victory
over Turkish invaders before the walls of Venice, September
12th, 1583.

What is the significance of the name of *Mary* that was,
under the direction of divine providence, given to the Virgin
Mother? Many devout persons have sought to answer this
question; one favourite explanation is that of St Bernard,
who says, 'Mary means *Stella maris*—Star of the sea', and in
an eloquent development of this idea, which is read in the
Breviary on September 12th, he shows that this name is most
becoming (*valde convenienter*) for the Blessed Virgin because
just as a star gives forth its light without any loss to itself, so
did the Mother of Jesus give birth to her Son without any
detriment to her virginity. On the other hand, St Peter
Chrysologus, in company with other Doctors of the Church,
says, in a passage also used in the office of this day (8th lesson),
Mary means 'Lady' or 'Princess'. According to this interpretation which, today, seems to the best exegetical scholars to be
the most likely, in calling upon the Mother of the Saviour by
her name of Mary we acknowledge at the same time, with
filial delicacy, our real dependence on the Queen of heaven
and earth even while still in this world.

In fact, the origin of the name of Mary is of little importance
to us, since it is the Blessed Virgin herself who gives it its true

significance. Mary is the name that, for us, calls to mind, more effectively than anything else, the thought of the Mother of our Saviour. In the eyes of the Church, the name of Mary sums up the whole mystery of the Blessed Virgin, just as the name of Jesus defines and embraces the entire work of our Lord. In celebrating the holy name of Mary, we pay homage to the Blessed Virgin herself, to her holiness, to the sum of her virtues, but above all to her purity. In honouring the name of Mary, we honour the Blessed Virgin as she was in the thought of God from the beginning; we acknowledge all the wonders that God has wrought in her and through her for the world's salvation; we delight in the fact that she reigns now and for evermore with Christ in the glory of heaven. But if the name of Mary recalls all her grandeur to us, it recalls also all the humiliations, all the suffering to which God's willing, humble and faithful handmaid submitted herself by giving herself to him. For as with the name of Jesus, so with the name of Mary. Today, no doubt, Jesus is the name of the risen and glorified Christ, but it recalls also, and always will, the memory of Bethlehem, of Nazareth and, above all, of Calvary, because it was precisely because of his obedience unto the death of the Cross that Christ became the 'Saviour'. The names of Jesus and Mary are henceforth inseparable from one another on the lips of Christians, because between them they sum up all the work wrought for our salvation by our Saviour and the Blessed Virgin his Mother.

The names of Jesus and Mary are not merely sweet to our taste, but are productive of sanctifying virtue, for these sacred names purify, justify and protect all those who pronounce them in a spirit of faith and love. In a certain way they communicate the virtue of the great mystery that they contain. Indeed it is not for nothing that the Church exhorts Christians, and especially the dying, to murmur constantly, until their dying breath, the saving names of 'Jesus' and 'Mary'.

Yes, the name of Mary tells us everything about the Virgin Mother, both her greatness and her virtue. It gives forth an exquisite and varied perfume. It tells of the humility and the prudence of our Lady, of her strength and her sweetness, but above all of her inviolable virginity. It is the 'Christian name' divinely chosen to designate the Blessed Virgin, and nobody but the Blessed Virgin, the Virgin of virgins, the Immaculate Virgin, the Virgin Mother of him who is virginity itself. It is enough for us that the name of Mary is that of the Mother of God, of the Queen who sits at our Lord's right hand in the glory of heaven, for us to give to this name such honour as so high a dignity deserves. Nevertheless it is chiefly the purity that shines forth from this name which compels us to invoke it with no less reverence than filial devotion. On the one hand, the name of Mary attracts us by the freshness and the grace which are its own; on the other, it makes us feel most vividly the insuperable distance that separates the Virgin of virgins from every other creature, even the angels themselves. In her liturgical prayer, notably at Mass, the Church never fails to designate the Virgin Mother by those glorious titles which commend her most to our veneration. Thus in the very heart of the Canon of the Mass, the *Communicantes*, the Church professes to 'venerate in the first place (*in primis*) the memory of the glorious Mary, ever a Virgin, Mother of God and of our Saviour Jesus Christ'. Moreover, real filial love never lapses into indiscreet and regrettable familiarity. In his encyclical *Ad coeli Reginam*, Pope Pius XII demands 'that the name of Mary, sweeter than nectar, more precious than any jewel, shall be the object of the greatest possible honours'.

CHAPTER IV

FEASTS OF DEVOTION

THE calendar of the universal Church shows many more feasts which, in the course of centuries but more particularly in modern times, have been instituted in honour of the Blessed Virgin. These feasts, which owe their existence to a variety of causes, all spring from that most legitimate sense of filial piety towards the Mother of God. Their manifest aim is to strengthen the confidence of Christian people in her sovereign protection, and to express our gratitude for all the benefits that so powerful an intercessor has obtained for us. However, since these feasts cannot possibly have, from the liturgical point of view, the interest of the great feasts of our Lady that we have already studied, we shall not spend long on them here. Moreover, it seems highly probable that liturgical reform on the lines of St Pius X's bull *Divino afflatus* may soon eliminate some of the feasts from the calendar of the universal Church, or at any rate reduce their liturgical rank.

First among these lesser solemnities, it is only right to place that feast which, in the universal Church, is celebrated under the curious name of the Dedication of Our Lady of the Snows. The antiquity of its institution, as well as its relative importance, naturally give it pride of place. This feast, too often passed by unnoticed these days, is actually the anniversary of the consecration of the most illustrious sanctuary of our Lady in Rome, St Mary Major's, which Pope Sixtus III restored and placed under the patronage of the Mother of God after the Council of Ephesus. In former chapters we have had more than one occasion to notice the liturgical importance of this basilica which, in the Missal, still bears the name of 'St Mary at the Crib', *Sancta Maria ad praesepe*, because it represents the place of Christ's birth at the heart of the Christian Church. It was here, in the days when the Pope went to the various 'stational' churches, that Christmas was always celebrated with great solemnity. St Mary Major's may well be called the liturgical centre for the cult of our Lady throughout the world. It is perfectly natural, therefore, that the universal Church should celebrate the anniversary of the dedication of St Mary Major's, just as she celebrates the dedication of the three other major basilicas of Rome—St John Lateran, St Peter's and St Paul's-outside-the-walls. It is a pity that the office for this 5th of August alludes only once, and that quite insignificantly, to the consecration of so great a church.

Like the feast just mentioned, that of the Presentation of the Blessed Virgin Mary goes back to a very early date, since it was celebrated at Jerusalem as far back as the sixth century. In the West it was not adopted until the fourteenth century, however, when Pope Gregory XI authorized its celebration at the court of Avignon in 1372. It was suppressed by St Pius V, but re-established by Sixtus V, extended to the whole Church in 1585 and raised to the rank of a major double. Benedict XIV only refrained from suppressing it again after much hesitation. The reason for this is, no doubt, the fact that the presentation of the Blessed Virgin in the temple has no historical background, but rests solely on an apocryphal legend. But it must be admitted that this feast of November 21st became very dear to Christian piety, since it celebrates not so much the more or less legendary presentation as such, but the Blessed Virgin as proposed in the antiphon for the *Magnificat* of the feast, that is, the true temple of the Lord, the sanctuary of the Holy Spirit: *Templum Domini, sacrarium Spiritus Sancti*. This it was that caused our Saviour Jesus Christ to take greater delight in her than in any other creature: *Sola sine exemplo placuisti Domino nostro Jesu Christo*. The recent feast (May 4th, 1944) of the Immaculate Heart of Mary, now celebrated on

August 22nd, connects up naturally with the Presentation, since it calls upon us to honour Mary as the worthy dwelling place of the Holy Spirit: *dignum Spiritus Sancti habitaculum.*

Modern Feasts

Of all the lesser feasts of the Blessed Virgin Mary, the one that seems to have acquired the greatest popularity among Christian people of our time is that of the Holy Rosary, celebrated on October 7th. Originally this feast was no more than a simple celebration for a confraternity, but after the famous victory over the Turks at Lepanto in 1571 which the Pope St Pius V himself attributed to the intercession of the Mother of God, its spread has never ceased down to our own day. Leo XIII devoted several encyclicals to the devotion of the rosary and raised its feast to the rank of Second Class, with Mass and office formerly peculiar to the Dominican Order. The feast of the Rosary calls upon the faithful to honour Mary in the share she had in the mysteries of Christ. The collect of the feast now used asks that fervent recitation of the rosary may obtain for us the grace to enter more deeply into the mysteries meditated upon and thence to profit by the fruit of them: *ut haec mysteria beatae Mariae Virginis rosario recolentes, et imitemur quod continent et quod promittunt assequamur.*

The Apparation of the Blessed Virgin Mary Immaculate (February 11th), instituted in memory of the miraculous appearances of our Lady at Lourdes, chiefly celebrates the Blessed Virgin in the privilege of her Immaculate Conception. The Maternity of the Blessed Virgin Mary (October 11th), after being suppressed by St Pius X, was restored by Pius XI in 1931 on the occasion of the fifteenth centenary of the Council of Ephesus which recognized the Mother of Christ as the true Mother of God. This feast, to speak frankly, is no more than a very faint commemoration of the great mystery that the Church celebrates already, in all its fulness and its proper liturgical framework, at Christmas time. Moreover, the anniversary of the dedication of St Mary Major's is surely more fitting as a memorial of the Council of Ephesus. The feast of our Lady's maternity has the further disadvantage of being celebrated a few days after that of the Rosary and, more strange still, the Gospel chosen for the feast is neither that of the Annunciation nor that of our Lord's birth.

To close the recent 'Marian Year' and as a perpetual memorial of it, Pope Pius XII instituted the feast of the Queenship of our Lady. In his encyclical *Ad coeli Reginam*, Pius XII declares that he has no intention of 'proposing some new truth to be believed, for the titles and arguments justifying the royal dignity of Mary have already been abundantly formulated in ancient documents of the Church and in liturgical books'. In the Pope's mind, this feast of Mary's royalty is instituted 'in order that all may recognize more clearly and honour with greater zeal the sweet and maternal empire of the Mother of God'. In this way, the Pope says, 'the feast can contribute much to preserve, consolidate and make permanent peace between peoples, threatened almost daily by disquieting events'.

Nothing need be said here about Our Lady of Mount Carmel (July 16th) and Our Lady of Ransom (September 24th). Both these feasts were originally peculiar to particular religious orders—the first to the Carmelites, the other to that of our Lady of Ransom founded for the redemption of captives. The Holy See only admitted them to the universal calendar very late and after much hesitation.

CHAPTER V

OUR LADY IN THE NON-FESTAL LITURGY

THE DAILY MASS AND OFFICE

IN the preceding chapters we have traced out our Lady's place in the liturgical year. But it goes without saying that the Church is not content to honour the motto of God only in those feasts more particularly consecrated to her. She is not even satisfied, during certain liturgical periods such as Advent, Christmastide, Epiphanytide, to place the Mother of the Redeemer in the most conspicuous place when celebrating those mysteries which she experienced in union with her Son for the salvation of the world. The Church, by her liturgy, seeks to keep us under the maternal patronage of our Lady every day of the year. Every day, the Holy Sacrifice is offered 'in honour of Blessed Mary ever a Virgin', that the sovereign power of her intercession may make itself known, as many prayers of the Mass recall. Special mention of her is found in the *Suscipe sancta Trinitas* just before the Secret; in the *Communicantes* of the Canon where in the first place (*in primis*) we venerate the memory of 'the glorious ever-virgin Mary, Mother of our God and Lord Jesus Christ'; and a third time in the prayer *Libera nos* which follows the *Paternoster*.

At the solemn hour of Vespers, the most important office of the day, the Church never omits our Lady's own canticle, the *Magnificat*, not even at the office for the dead or the last days of Holy Week. Neither does the Church ever conclude the daily office by the solemn celebration of Compline without invoking the Blessed Virgin Mary in one or other of the beautiful antiphons which are familiar to us all, and which vary according to the liturgical season. The *Alma Redemptoris* embraces Advent and Christmastide, beginning on the eve of the first Sunday in Advent and ending with the feast of the Presentation on February 2nd. In this antiphon, the Church calls upon the glorious Mother of the Redeemer—'Star of the sea and gate of heaven'—to succour our fallen race as it strives to rise. For this Mother is all powerful, who, to the amazement of nature (*natura mirante*), brought forth her own Creator, remaining a Virgin after childbearing as she was before. From Compline on February 2nd until that of Wednesday in Holy Week, the office ends with the *Ave Regina caelorum*, a charming antiphon of six lines, containing some delightful rhyming, which salutes the Blessed Mother as 'Queen of heaven and Mistress of the angels, root of Jesse and gate through which came the Light of the world'. While congratulating the 'glorious Virgin, beautiful above all others'—*Gaude, Virgo gloriosa super omnes speciosa*—it implores her intercession with Christ on our behalf. During the fifty days of Eastertide, the joyful *Regina caeli* bids us share in the gladness felt by the Queen of heaven when the Son whom it had been her privilege to bear in her womb rose again from the dead. But the best known of all these four antiphons is the *Salve Regina*, being, as it certainly is, the most beautiful and the most moving. Since it deserves a fuller study than the other three, both because of its doctrinal wealth and its earnest supplication, we shall treat of it specially at the end of this book.

These four antiphons found their way into the Roman liturgy in 1350 thanks to the Franciscan Friars Minor, in whose breviary they had had a place since 1249.

The Little Office of the Blessed Virgin

The office entitled *Officium parvum B Mariae Virginis*, the Little Office of the Blessed Virgin Mary, is still to be found in the Roman Breviary. Little is known about the origin of this daily office which, in the course of the Middle Ages, was added regularly to the singing of the canonical office. We know that about the middle of the ninth century, perhaps in the Camaldolese abbey of Fonte Avellano, the daily public recitation of the Little Office of our Lady was introduced. Its institution has often been attributed to St Peter Damian who, before he became a Cardinal and Bishop of Ostia, had been a monk of Fonte Avellano. His responsibility for it seems highly doubtful, but there is every probability that he had a large share in popularizing this office, since he warmly recommends its daily recitation in his work *De horis canonicis* (P.L. 145, 230). From the eleventh century onwards the daily recitation of the Hours of our Lady spread rapidly in France, Germany, England, and even in Rome, where there are traces of its being used in the Lateran basilica in the twelfth century. With the exception of certain greater feasts, both the secular and the regular clergy became obliged to the daily recitation of this Little Office until St Pius V, in his reform of the Roman breviary, made it optional. A few congregations of religious still add the recitation of our Lady's Office to the Canonical Office, and not a few modern institutes and communities recite it in place of the office of the day.

'*Our Lady of Saturday*'

In the early Church, Saturday was a day of fasting both in Rome and elsewhere. It was not until the ninth century that a tendency showed itself to consecrate this day to the memory of the Blessed Virgin. The monk Alcuin, in the ninth century, introduced seven votive Masses into the Roman Sacramentary, one for each day of the week. The last of the series was *De sancta Maria*, which leads one to suppose that this was reserved for Saturday, the day more specially consecrated already to our Lady. Very little is known as to the origin of the office of our Lady which the Church uses on every Saturday not taken up by some feast. The most ancient text of this office is supposed to be in the Customary of the abbey of Einsiedeln (tenth century). At all events, since the reform of St Pius V (sixteenth century), this office *De Beata* is fortunately combined with that of the day. The psalms are those of Saturday and the first two lessons are from the ferial lessons for that day; the third being taken from some writing of the Fathers. The rest of the office is from the Common of our Lady.

Corresponding regularly with this Saturday office is a Mass in honour of our Lady, varying according to the seasons of the liturgical year. There are five to be found in the Roman Missal. The first is for use in Advent, with its 'Proper' and readings from the Ember Wednesday of Advent, the famous *Missus est*. From Christmas to Candlemas, the Epistle and Gospel are taken from the Mass of the Dawn of Christmas Day and the prayers are from the feast of the Circumcision. From Easter until Pentecost, the Gospel tells us of Christ giving us, from his Cross, in the person of St John, his own Mother as ours. For the few Saturdays between February 2nd and Lent, the Mass is little different from that in normal use after Pentecost. As on all feasts of our Lady, so on these Saturdays also, the Church provides the Mass with a Proper Preface which brings out, with as much delicacy as precision, the eminent dignity of her who, while maintaining the glory of her virginity, gave birth to the Light of the world, our Lord Jesus Christ—*et virginitatis gloria permanente, lumen aeternum mundo effudit, Jesum Christum Dominum nostrum*. The Preface of the Blessed Virgin as we have it was originally sung in Gaul for the feast of the Assumption. Alcuin modified it and inserted it in his supplement to the Gregorian Sacramentary. In 1085, Pope Urban II modified it still further so as to make it suitable for all feasts of our Lady, and this is the form of it that we still have. Thanks to modern simplification of the Roman calendar, we shall soon have the joy of seeing most Saturdays in the year devoted to the celebration of an Office and Mass in honour of the Mother of God.

CONCLUSION

IF we would be the faithful children of our Blessed Lady, our devotion to her should be extremely simple, spontaneous, one might almost say natural. It should not be encumbered with a mass of words or an accumulation of little practices which we perform with more or less attention according to our feelings on any particular day. Fundamentally it should consist in a deeply sincere attitude of soul, a certain orientation of the mind and the heart by which we live in our Lady's sight, like the child that lives freely and joyfully under the watchful care of his mother. True devotion to the Blessed Virgin is shown by an habitual and lively sense of her presence, of her tenderness, of her protection; by an irresistible need to have recourse to her in the smallest details of our daily life, and especially in our temptations, our sufferings and our trials. To acquire such dispositions, there is no surer way than to live the life of the Church and make her prayer our own.

The great danger to which modern devotion to our Lady is exposed is, as M. Laurentin declares, 'to cut the Blessed Virgin off from those theological realities in the midst of which she resides'. According to our yielding to this temptation so will our devotion go awry; doctrine and piety become 'closed shops' . . . Marian theology is tempted to become 'Mariology' and devotion to Mary to become 'Mariolatry'. The same author points out specially two deviations which threaten the true devotion that we ought to have for the Mother of God: superficial piety and unbalanced piety. Superficial piety is formalism that consists in multiplying external practices without giving our heart and mind to it. M. Laurentin gives the following concrete examples: 'It is easier to get people to sign a petition for the institution of some new liturgical feast or for some definition about our

Lady, than it is to observe in a worthy manner those feasts which already exist, or to make a serious study of established dogmas. To this we may add that anxiety to swell certain statistics leads sometimes to most disagreable procedures. One could wish that in certain "Marian" organizations today there was more moderation on one side and a greater interior and spiritual effort on the other. This is not to condemn out of hand every external and popular aspect of deveotion to our Lady, but rather to integrate variety into unity and recognize that the value of devotions springs from within.'

Devotion to the Mother of God is not only too frequently superficial, but tends sometimes to excess arising out of a false conception of her share in the economy of salvation. 'Too many efforts are made', says M. Laurentin, 'to propagate the unique rule *De Maria nunquam satis*, while it is forgotten that the important thing is to give Mary her true place in relation to Christ and the Church. From this there results an unbalanced appreciation of Christian values and a certain uneasiness felt in the presence of efforts that are keen and sincere but which develop in a way that is foreign to Christian equipoise.'

But souls whose devotion to our Lady is nourished by the Church's own prayer, as from a most pure spring, are certainly shielded from those regrettable deviations just spoken of by an author whose experience in such matters is beyond cavil. Besides the very large place allocated to the cult of the Blessed Virgin by the Church, the liturgy is of a nature to satisfy every demand of a truly filial devotion towards her. This being so, it appears to us regrettable, not to say inopportune, to wish to multiply inconsiderately feasts of our Lady on the pretext of honouring her further and promoting filial piety towards her. As an eminent modern liturgist, Dom B. Botte, has so rightly said, 'If feasts are multiplied endlessly, the very idea of a feast day ends by disappearing, with all that it suggests in the way of solemnity'. Moreover, new feasts cannot go on multiplying without detriment to the old which are, most often, not only more venerable but of far greater

F

importance in the liturgical cycle. Again, the multiplication of feasts seriously upsets the balance of the calendar, breeds monotony and hinders the celebration of the Sunday Office which the wise reforms of St Pius X had precisely aimed at restoring.

Finally, 'What we must avoid', writes M. Laurentin, 'is letting the ardour of our love make our Blessed Lady the be-all and end-all of our spiritual life. This would be to materialize that pure soaring flight by which she herself ever tends towards God and draws us to him with her; this could only dull the appreciation of her mediation on our behalf and place a screen between us and God.' For indeed, our Lady's lot is not to hide Christ from us, but on the contrary to show him to us. If therefore we would keep that filial freshness in our devotion to our Lady that springs from true simplicity, we must above all be on our guard against divorcing it from the worship that we offer to her Son, our Lord Jesus Christ. As we said at the beginning of this little work, the mysteries of Mary are the mysteries of Jesus and her glory is the reflection of his glory.

Pictures and statues of our Lady that speak most eloquently to the Christian soul are those that depict the Virgin Mother holding the Son of her virginity in her arms, to give him to us. In religious art of the Middle Ages, one rarely finds pictures or statues of the Blessed Mother without her Son, either in her arms or on her lap, as though enthroned. It was left for modern times, under the influence of our Lady's appearing at various places, to produce solitary figures of her. Yet it seems a pity to abandon the medieval practice whose theological meaning was clear to all. Moreover, at a time when Marian theology was less developed than it is today, our ancestors owed to the liturgy, in which their minds were steeped, that solid and delicate piety towards the Virgin Mother which, in the sphere of art and letters, has left us so many masterpieces.

APPENDIX

THE 'SALVE REGINA'

A MODEL OF PRAISE AND SUPPLICATION

THE *Salva Regina* is not, as was once thought, the work of Adhemar de Monteil, Bishop of le Puys (†1098), nor of St Bernard, who knew it and popularized it. Today it is attributed, with considerable probability, to Hermann Contract, monk of Reichenau Abbey, who died in 1054. He also composed the *Alma Redemptoris*. It is not known exactly when the *Salve Regina* was introduced into the liturgy. In the twelfth century it was used as the Benedictus antiphon for certain feasts of our Lady. The Dominicans were probably the first to sing the *Salve* after Compline, about 1221. In 1239, Pope Gregory IX, on the advice of St Raymond of Pennafort, ordered it to be sung in Rome on Friday evenings. In the royal chapel of St Louis it was sung daily after Compline, and in the course of the thirteenth century it became popular all over the Western Church. In certain monastic orders—Benedictines, Cistercians, Carmelites and Dominicans—its singing after Compline is treated with no small solemnity.

There is no doubt that of the four beautiful antiphons of our Lady nowadays incorporated in the divine office, the favourite among our forefathers was certainly the *Salve Regina*. In the Roman rite it is sung at the end of Compline from the end of Paschaltide until Advent, that is to say for six months of the year. Originally, it was the only antiphon sung at the end of Compline, as is still the case in the Cistercian Order. Our forefathers' predilection for the *Salve Regina* is easy to understand. Doubtless, the other three, *Alma Redemp-*

toris, *Ave Regina caelorum* and *Regina caeli*, are beautiful invocations of our Lady, but none has the deep tenderness of the *Salve*, none is so suppliant, so moving. It is a cry from the heart, the heart of one who knows the meaning of deep distress. It is the cry of children to their Mother in the midst of tribulation and anxiety. Truly the *Salve* is the most pure expression of the piety of the Middle Ages towards our Lady, a piety that is simple, full of confidence, wholly spontaneous, completely foreign to the often complicated and subtle forms of modern piety. It is a product of the age when Christianity dedicated its most glorious cathedrals to the Blessed Virgin and yielded a profusion of the most expressive and noble statues of the Virgin Mother bearing the Christ-child in her arms.

The Salutation of the Blessed Virgin

The antiphon begins with a salutation: *Salve*. Is not this exactly the way in which loving sons should greet their Mother? Before giving her his message from the Most High God, the angel Gabriel began by saluting the Blessed Virgin, *Ave gratia plena*. Elizabeth, when she saw the Virgin Mother hastening towards her, saluted her and proclaimed her blessed: *Benedicta tu inter mulieres*. How frequently do the Church's invocations of our Blessed Lady begin with a gracious salutation: *Ave Regina caelorum*, *Ave maris Stella*, *Salve sancta Parens*. . . .

Salve Regina—'Hail, holy Queen'! Yes, the Virgin Mother is a queen indeed, and it was most advisedly that medieval art used to place a crown on precious stones upon her head. No doubt, so long as she lived on earth, she was no more than a handmaid, the little handmaid of the Lord, *ancilla Domini*. Hers was the humility and the devotion of a submissive and faithful servant. In this way she shared the lot of her own Son, who dispoiled himself of the glories of his divinity and took upon himself the form of a servant, *in forma servi*, obedient in all things unto the death of the Cross. But, again like her Son, and following in his footsteps, Mary has herself passed to the state of glory. From being the humble handmaid that she was on earth, she has become our Queen in heaven. She only experienced death so that she might rise again and be taken up to heaven to sit at the right hand of Christ. For many centuries now the liturgy of the Assumption has proclaimed this royalty of the Blessed Virgin Mary: *Hodie Maria Virgo caelos ascendit, gaudete quia cum Christo regnat in aeternum* (2nd Vespers *Magnificat* antiphon).

On the day of his glorious Ascension, Christ became 'Lord', 'our Lord'. When, in her turn, Mary was glorified, she became 'Lady', 'our Lady', so that the Church ever delights in recognizing her royalty, and calls upon her as Queen of heaven, *Regina caelorum*, Queen of angels, of apostles, of martyrs, of virgins, of all the saints. Together with her Son, the Blessed Virgin enjoys a universal royalty, and a royalty that is not merely honorary but effective. As the new Esther, she is sovereign by her intercession. Since she has been crowned in heaven, her intercession is that of a Queen. Enjoying total and eminently efficacious power over the heart of Christ and disposing as she will of all the fruits of his Passion because of her co-operation in the work of our redemption, our Lady is the mediatrix of all graces.

Mater misericordiae, 'Mother of mercy'. The primitive text of the *Salve* had '*Regina misericordiae*', Queen of mercy. And indeed Mary is the Queen of mercy, because her all-powerful intercession is ever exercised in favour of mercy. However, the custom has prevailed of calling her 'Mother of mercy', which is even more forceful, since this title underlines more the part of our Lady in the divine work. The Redemption is a work of mercy. Creation shows forth the goodness of God. But mercy implies something more than goodness. It is goodness poured out on wretchedness. Mercy is only for the wretched, the unfortunate. Was it not to show forth the excess of his mercy that God permitted the Fall of man? If there had been no sin, there would have been no redemption, no mercy. Hence the audacious exclamation of the *Exultet* at the Easter Vigil: *O felix culpa*, 'O happy fault!' Our Lady is truly the Mother of mercy since she only exists for a merciful purpose. As Terrien says, in his *La Mère des Hommes*, 'She is the queen of angels, and yet God gave her not to the angels but to sinful man'. From this springs her compassion, her attraction for sinners for whom she is the supreme refuge, *Refugium peccatorum*. To touch her maternal heart, we have only to acknowledge ourselves sinners, *ora pro nobis peccatoribus*.

The Blessed Virgin is in a most real sense the Mother of mercy because, by her virginal conceiving, she gave us the author of all mercy, him who St Paul calls 'our Redemption' (I Cor. 1, 30). It was precisely through taking our flesh in the womb of the Blessed Virgin that Christ became 'merciful and compassionate' in the fullest meaning of the words (Heb. 2, 17). It was from the Blessed Virgin alone that he received that human heart which the Church honours as the seat, or at least the symbol, of infinite mercy.

Vita, 'our life'—this is even more surprising. Has not our Lord himself declared that he, and he alone, is the life—'I am the Way, the Truth and the Life' (John 14, 6)? Indeed, he is the Life, he who became in his humanity the source of our supernatural life. Do we not exaggerate somewhat, therefore, in attributing this name to our Lady? The primitive text of the *Salve* read *vitae dulcedo*, 'the sweetness of life', a phrase both charming and true. Yet the Church does not fear to go a stage further, calling her, like her Son, just 'our life'. This presupposes between Christ and his Mother a union closer than we can conceive in any other circumstances. If our Lord is for us the source of divine life, we know that he never pours it forth without the intervention of our Lady—for it was she who gave him to us, with all that he is or has. So she has a kind of right over all that Christ acquired by virtue of his blood. It is truly from her that we have received the author of life; it is by her that we have merited this favour, as we say in the collect for her office at Christmastide: *Per quam meruimus auctorem vitae suscipere*. If Christ is the source of life for us, he is so in his humanity, and that humanity he has from Mary.

He is the fruit of her womb. So she is truly our life, she enters into our life, we cannot live without her. Life comes to us from Christ, but through the instrumentality of Mary and thanks to her.

Dulcedo, 'our sweetness'. Sweetness is the first idea to come into our minds at the mention of the name of Mary. We love to utter that name because of its sweetness. We always think of our Lady as a young woman, with gracious and most pure features, and an expression of incomparable sweetness. For the Church, Mary is the personification of sweetness, *dulcedo*. In the hymn *Ave maris Stella*, she is said to be *inter omnes mitis* —'sweet above all other', and we ask her to let us share in her own sweetness, *nos mites fac et castos*. There are shades of meaning in the two Latin words *dulcis* and *mitis* which do not lend themselves easily to translation.

Dulcis is the sweetness that is the opposite of bitterness, harshness, or sharpness. It is the word used for an agreeable fruit. Used for a person, it suggests charm and suavity of manner, the sweetness of a smile that wins people's hearts. Such is our Lady's sweetness that we invoke under the gracious title of *Mater amabilis*, and of whom it is said that her spirit is sweeter than honey: *Spiritus meus super mel dulcis* (Eccl. 24, 27).

Mitis is that sweetness that is opposed to hardness of heart and stiffness of manner. It is sweetness expressed by tenderness, forbearance, goodness, and implies true humility since the proud are usually hard of heart. Humility and sweetness always go together. Scripture puts the humble and sweet-natured people (*mitis*) in the same category. In the Sermon on the Mount, Christ declared them blessed, and gave himself to us as being 'meek and humble of heart' (Matt. 11, 29).

There is yet a third Latin term that expresses equally well the sweetness of our Lady—*mansuetus*. This form of sweetness is opposed to what is savage, fierce and violent. Applied to man, it indicates an accessible character, welcoming and very human. Now if our Lady is the highest, the most sublime of all creatures to such a degree that, as Cajetan says, 'she borders on the divinity', she is also the most welcoming, the most human of creatures, like her Son Jesus Christ who, the most human of men, delighted to call himself 'the Son of man'.

In all respects, then, the Blessed Virgin Mary is truly the personification of sweetness, *dulcedo*. She is the Mother of him who was the most gentle of men, the Mother of the Lamb of God, who was led to the slaughter without opening his mouth. In all the mysteries of her life, and especially at Bethlehem and Nazareth, Mary is seen as the most perfect expression of maternal sweetness. She is 'our sweetness'; the thought of her, the image of her, her invisible presence, all diffuse her sweetness, radiate her sweetness. It is good to dwell on this in this present age, when so much hardness and bitterness never tire of inventing new refinements of cruelty. Let us look to our Mother and ask her to obtain for us that sweetness which St Paul numbers among the fruits of the Holy Spirit, and which is truly the perfume of the most exquisite charity. Sweetness joined to strength, which in our Lady had no connection with sentimentality and softness.

Spes nostra, 'our hope'. Again, is it an exaggeration to call the Blessed Virgin 'our hope'? Is not Christ and Christ alone both the motive and the object of Christian hope? Yet Mary too has the right to be called 'our hope'. In a passage of Scripture which the Church places on our Lady's lips (Eccl. 24, 24), she calls herself the 'Mother of holy hope', *Mater sanctae spei*. Many are the churches in the world that are dedicated to 'our Lady of Good Hope'. Christ is indeed our hope, but you cannot separate the Mother from the Son. Mary gave us Christ, and with Christ has restored to us that hope which by sin we had lost. The day that our Lady was born into this world was the day on which joy and hope were born again with her. A further reason for calling her our hope is the fact that she is our Mother and a Mother who is all-powerful. Her intercession is sovereignly efficacious. She is the Mother of mercy, the Star that shines out in the blackest night. When all seems lost, she is still there. We are sure of her mercy, her tenderness. She is like our last refuge. She is all that we mean by 'mother', the person to whom every man turns in his most

dire distress and whom he calls upon instinctively in the hour
of peril.

Salve . . . Salve . . . Salve. After this touching greeting that
must immediately touch the heart of the Virgin Mother there
follow the cries of distress that rise up to the Mother of mercy.

The Earnest Supplication

Ad te clamamus, exules, filii Hevae, 'To thee we cry, poor
banished children of Eve'. It is indeed a cry, *clamamus*, the
heart-rending cry uttered in the hour of extreme distress, that
springs from the depths of our being. Mary dwells in the
height of heaven; we, poor things, are on earth; an abyss
separates us. We cry out to her like some wretch who has
fallen down a precipice cries aloud to his rescuer whom he sees
afar off.

Exules, 'exiles', 'banished'—we know only too well that we
are! We remain in banishment, in exile, until we return to our
fatherland, our Father's land, that is to say heaven, where we
ought already to be living in spirit and in heart, as St Paul bids
us: *conversatio nostra in caelis est* (Phil. 3, 20). But the further we
advance in this present life, the more we become aware of our
exile. We understand more and more clearly the deceptive
frailty of all things here below. We see more vividly the
ephemeral and transitory condition of our earthly existence.
Years seem to slip away with ever growing speed as their
term approaches. Daily, things that bind us to earth disappear.
Our parents are taken from us, then our friends also; one by
one they all enter their eternity. We have only to glance back
over the years to see how many blank spaces! We feel we are
being urged on by some invisible power. We are passing
away. It is our exile. Even our memories vanish. If we return
to some place where we used to spend our childhood, we no
longer find anything there that we formerly knew and loved.
Even the old house we lived in has gone. In a few years, all
has been changed, all spoiled. Only in the cemetery do we
find names that we knew. Today more than ever, the tragic
and warlike course of events, the instability of institutions,

the mobile nature of our very existence makes us feel most acutely our condition of exiles and pilgrims. True saints are filled with nostalgia for heaven, but we, in this mortal body, we are in exile, far from the Lord, as St Paul says: *Dum sumus in corpore peregrinamur a Domino* (II Cor. 5, 6). How frequently do we find the sorrows of exile deeply expressed in the psalms!

Filii Hevae: Although Mary is our Mother according to grace, we none the less remain by nature the dependants of the first woman, since we still have within us the results of original sin. Our whole inheritance of misery that we bear with us in this world comes down to us from our first mother. We almost subtly recall this fact to the Blessed Virgin so as to stir within her a certain maternal jealousy, so that she may hasten to substitute her influence for that of the first Eve.

Ad te suspiramus, gementes et flentes in hac lacrymarum valle, 'To thee do we send up our signs, mourning and weeping in this vale of tears'. Note the three verbs expressing our grief, our anxiety—*suspiramus, gementes et flentes*. Sighs, mourning, weeping. Such is our prayer to the Blessed Mother. Indeed the Bible itself speaks of the place of our dwelling as a 'valley of tears' (Ps. 83, 6). For this earth is no more than a fleeting place of exile, filled with sorrows. How deceptive and ephemeral are the joys of this life, and on the other hand, how many are its cares and pains, its anxieties and troubles of all sorts. We have only to look round on the world so recently turned upside down by the cruellest of wars and still threatened by further disasters.

Eja ergo, advocata nostra, illos tuos misericordes oculos ad nos converte, 'Turn then, most gracious advocate, thine eyes of mercy towards us'. *Advocata nostra*—most gracious advocate —Mary is surely this in her quality as Mother, Mother of mercy. The Blessed Virgin is an excessively good Mother. Whatever the wretchedness, the disgrace of her sons, whatever their crimes and their falls, a true mother can never condemn them, never exclude them from her love. The most perverse, the most guilty, the most sin-stained soul in the world has only to stand before the Blessed Virgin and she will find there something to love. She knows the price of souls, and only sees them covered with the precious blood of her Son, so she has it much at heart to snatch them from the devil. In the Apocalypse, the devil is portrayed as the perpetual accuser, *Accusator fratrum nostrorum.* Night and day, he rises up and accuses us before God, *qui accusabat illos ante conspectum Dei, die ac nocte* (Apoc. 12, 10). He deceives souls, urges them on to do evil, and then demands their damnation. Mary, who in all respects is the declared adversary of the spirit of evil, does exactly the opposite. Hers is the part of the advocate, she protects and defends us. She protects us against temptation and defends us against the fiery darts of the tempter, his suggestions and his traps. But if by some misfortune we have fallen victims of our own weakness, she intercedes with the Lord for our pardon, she prays for 'us sinners' and helps us to rise up again. Assuredly, God's judgment seat is not like those on earth. In heaven, there is neither plaintiff nor counsel for the defence, and the sentence is immediate. But at a death-bed, before some soul goes forth to stand before the Sovereign Judge, there is sometimes a sharp struggle between the Blessed Virgin and the devil. This is recognized in the prayers that the Church provides for use at the bedside of the dying (cf. *Ritus*). Our Lady's part at the death of sinners is most mysterious. Who can tell the wonders that are wrought by her intercession at that moment? Surely she sees to it that the merits of Christ and the pains of his Passion are not in vain. And when the soul has gone forth from this world, will she not still be there to plead the cause of those suffering the purifying pains of Purgatory?

Ad nos converte. Why should we ask our Lady this, when we know that her regard is ever upon us? She never lets her attention to us wander. Nothing that concerns us escapes her. This we know from the theological principle which holds that those in heaven see by means of the light of glory every-thing that they have a legitimate desire to know, all that could interest them here below. This sight of theirs is perfectly

clear, without any created intermediary. Is it not evident that
the Blessed Virgin Mary, being our Mother in the order of
grace, must have a perfect knowledge of everything that
concerns the life of souls? She sees all, our miseries, our least
sins, our temptations. None the less, we must implore her aid
at those moments when we are most aware of our own
weakness, even if this is to do no more than pay our homage
to her motherly kindness; just as we pray to God, not to
inform him of our needs, for he knows them better than we
do, but to pay homage to his Fatherhood.

*Et Jesum benedictum fructum ventris tui, nobis post hoc exilium
ostende*, 'And after this our exile, show us the blessed fruit of
thy womb, Jesus'. We can ask our Lady for no greater grace
than that. In fact we are asking her to lead us through the
difficulties, temptations and dangers, of our exile, until we
come to the vision of Jesus, the blessed fruit of her womb. Is
not this just what we ask in the hymn *Ave maris Stella?*

> *Iter para tutum*
> *Ut videntes Jesum*
> *Semper collaetemur.*

All the favours that our Lady obtains for us are summed up
in this supreme grace; to enjoy the blessed vision of our
Saviour. This is the highest of graces, since it is a matter of
nothing less than final perseverance, that is, fidelity until the
last moment of our life. Are we not constantly recommending
this supreme moment to the care of our Blessed Mother, *ora
pro nobis . . . in hora mortis nostrae?*

In the *Salve Regina*, with what grace and filial piety is this
request proffered. First, in the Latin, comes the name that ever
fills the Blessed Mother with joy, *Jesum*, 'Jesus, the blessed fruit
of thy womb', re-echoing the words of Elizabeth at the
Visitation. Then, as we so constantly recall to her, Jesus is the
fruit of her flesh and blood, but also the fruit of her holiness,
her humility, her obedience. He is the Son of her virginity.
He is the fruit of her sufferings also, since she brought him
forth a second time for our salvation by uniting herself to his
Passion on Calvary. Jesus is everything to the Blessed Virgin.

He is her fruit, her offspring, destined to save the world, the fruit of life. *Per te fructum vitae communicavimus*, 'By thee, we have received the fruit of life' (4th Ant. Lauds of the Assumption).

Nobis post hoc exilium ostende. It is for the Blessed Virgin to lead us to Christ and show him to us. When the first Eve had tasted the forbidden fruit, she offered it to Adam, who ate it for his own death. Mary shows herself as the new Eve, the true Mother of all the living, by giving us with her motherly hands that fruit which brings life, Jesus, so that he may be our eternal nourishment in heaven.

The antiphon ends with the most moving triple invocation: *O clemens*, 'O clement'. In the Canon of the Mass we address God the Father as '*Clementissime Pater*, but Mary, in her motherhood, is the most pure reflection of the indulgent goodness of the Father. *O pia.* The word is scarcely translatable. *Pius* in Latin means profound and merciful kindness and charity. In the doxologies of hymns, the Church constantly addresses God the Father as *Pater piissiumus*. What could be more suitable to the Blessed Virgin, who is Mother of God's Son? *O dulcis Virgo Maria*, 'O sweet Virgin Mary'. Once again, sweetness. Then the last word, 'Mary'. On this name, uttered with unspeakable love, this name that gathers up all, that is enough in itself, the antiphon ends. It is the last word, the last shaft to touch the Blessed Virgin's heart and make her bend down to us.